Amazing

NEWFOUNDLAND STORIES
From Jack Fitzgerald's Notebook

Amazing

NEWFOUNDLAND STORIES
From Jack Fitzgerald's Notebook

CREATIVE PUBLISHERS
St. John's, Newfoundland
1986

Cover: Maurice Fitzgerald

1st printing November 1986
2nd printing August 1987
3rd printing June 1988
4th printing December 1988
5th printing July 1991
6th printing November 1997
7th printing June 1999
8th printing June 2000
9th printing April 2001

∞ Printed on acid-free paper

Published by

CREATIVE BOOK PUBLISHING

a division of 10366 Newfoundland Limited
a Robinson-Blackmore Printing & Publishing associated company
P.O. Box 8660, St. John's, Newfoundland A1B 3T7

Printed in Canada by:
ROBINSON-BLACKMORE PRINTING & PUBLISHING

ISBN 0-920021-25-5

Introduction

Jack Fitzgerald's Notebook is a collection of unusual, amazing, offbeat and intriguing stories from Newfoundland's past. This book contains stories of mystery, Newfoundland heroes, crimes both ancient and modern, as well as unique and interesting miscellany.

The material for this book was gathered from tons of records preserved at the Provincial Archives and the Newfoundland Historical Society. Some stories were gathered from story tellers and from part of our Newfoundland folklore.

While most of the material is historically correct and easily verified other parts, especially those stories handed down from generation to generation, are not as easily confirmed.

Nevertheless, all stories are a valuable part of our Newfoundland legends, folklore and history and I hope the reader will find them as interesting and entertaining as I did in gathering them.

Dr. Robbie Robertson deserves special thanks for her endless patience and co-operation in helping me track down material for the book and for her outstanding work for the Newfoundland Historical Society in maintaining her up to date and exhaustive filing records.

Chapter I

STRANGE STORIES

This chapter deals with some of the strange, the unusual, and the unexplained stories from the offbeat but colorful history of Newfoundland. Stories like the mystery Devil Ship, the waterfalls from the sky, the jinxed ship and a truly unusual funeral service make for gripping and fascinating reading.

A Strange Phenomenon
The Jinxed Ship
The Sabrina
Louise Journeaux
The Meteorite
The Devil Ship
Monuments and Graves
A Spectacular Sky Show
Giant Squid
Two Amazing Stories
Curious Event
A West Coast Mystery
A Perilous Feat
A Mystery Find at Bay Bulls

A Strange Phenomenon

A terrifying incident in waters between Port aux Basques and Sydney caused Bob Strickland to comment, "I've crossed the Gulf hundreds of times but never saw anything like it before."

"And," shipmate Alex Chaisson added, "I never want to see it again!"

The two seamen were crew members of the 47 ton schooner *Cedella* that on October 3, 1909 encountered one of the rarest and most remarkable phenomenon ever to occur at sea. Strickland, the *Cedella*'s mate later described the event saying, "I never did see the sky so thick and low before." They were about 35 miles east of Cape Breton at the time.

Chaisson was the first man to spot the strange happening. He said, "All of a sudden we saw a pillar of water falling out of the sky about a mile away. It was moving straight towards us and as the water was falling down, the sea was soaring high. It looked like a funnel, big at the top and narrow at the bottom. All around it the waves were swirling like a whirlpool. The thing itself kept twisting around and around."

The skipper ordered the crew to get the sails down as soon as possible. They had it reefed in seconds. No sooner did they have the canvas all folded away, than the whirlwind of water suddenly moved in and encircled the ship.

Adding to the terror of the men was the unexpected fog that quickly moved over the whole area. They could not see the swirling water through the fog but they could hear it.

Then, as suddenly as it had appeared, the fog lifted and the waterfalls disappeared. As they moved on toward Cape Breton they could see similar phenomena off in the distance. Many other vessels in the St. Lawrence that day reported seeing the same phenomena.

What was it they had seen? Scientists identified it as a series of waterspouts similar to a tornado. It was the first time that waterspouts had been seen north of the twenty-second parallel, located around the West Indies. It was an experience those witnesses would never forget.

The Jinxed Ship

The famous *Great Eastern* that laid the first trans-Atlantic telegraph cable at Heart's Content was jinxed. On her maiden voyage, she carried a crew of 400, but only 36 passengers. The vessel had a capacity to handle 4,000 passengers, and the venture proved costly to the owners.

During the launching, seven men were killed and several others seriously injured. The original captain and the purser's son both died in that mishap.

A few hours out to sea, the engines broke down, and the Captain ordered the sails raised. They failed to move the ship and were lowered, never to be raised again. The engines were repaired but broke down again, and it took another three days before repairs were completed. On June 27, 1860 the *Great Eastern* arrived at New York and, while being greeted by thousands of well-wishers and a fourteen-gun salute, crashed against the pier causing damage to the pierhead.

After docking, two stokers got drunk, fell overboard, and drowned. A deckhand went mad during the Atlantic crossing; and, on the first night in New York, a fight broke out among the crew which left one man dead.

Early the next morning, the ship's navigator was found dead in his room, from alcohol poisoning.

A real tragedy occurred when the *Great Eastern* broke into flames at the New York Dock. Both the New York Fire Department and the Harbour Fire Department fought among themselves for the honour of putting out the fire. During the confrontation five men were shot, three were axed to death, and several were clubbed and left in serious condition. While the firemen fought and killed each other, the crew of the *Great Eastern* managed to put out the fire.

In an effort to raise money, the owners opened the vessel to sightseers at one dollar per head. The visitors stole everything; including the silverware, paintings, and even mattresses from the beds. A ship's officer who tried to stop the looters was knocked unconscious and a crew member was badly beaten.

The owners again tried to raise money, this time by offering a two-day cruise at ten dollars per head. Two thousand passengers booked on for the trip from New York to Cape May, New Jersey, and return. When the paddle wheels were started, they stirred up the mud and brought the two drowned stokers to the surface. The owners expected to make money on the bar, but the passengers brought their own liquor. Poker games were being played all over the ship and there were many brawls.

All hell broke loose when the 2,000 passengers began looking for lunch in the dining room only to learn that there was no food available. The caterer, who had been paid in advance, skipped New York without supplying the food and the ship's crew had failed to check it out before departure. At bed-time there were only 300 mattresses for 2,000 passengers; so most slept on deck until a rainstorm broke out.

Well, at least they were near Cape May, — or so they thought. However, during the night the ship had drifted 200 miles off course, and was out in the Atlantic!

After a lengthy delay, she finally reached port and four men were killed during the stampede to get ashore.

"The Great Eastern"
Courtesy — Provincial Archives, Nfld.

The Sabrina

A funeral service that was among the most unusual ever to take place in all Canada took place over Gander airport on the morning of September 23, 1946. Aboard the aircraft, conducting the service, was the Roman Catholic Bishop of Central Newfoundland, Bishop McGrath; and the manager of the Belgian Sabrina Airlines, Gilbert Perrier. Among the curious spectators at the Gander airport terminal, which had officially opened only a few days earlier, was Hollywood movie star, George Sanders, who portrayed the Saint in a series of Hollywood movies.

The unusual funeral ceremony was being held for the victims of a passenger plane crash 22 miles from Gander airport in a wooded area so thick that authorities decided to build a cemetery at the crash site rather than risk lives in bringing out the victims.

The tragedy occurred when the Skymaster aircraft with 45 people on board was getting ready to touch down at Gander for refueling during a flight from Shannon, Ireland to New York. Just after issuing permission for the Belgian plane to land, the tower at Gander lost contact with the aircraft and emergency measures were quickly put into effect. Search planes from both the United States and Canadian Forces were sent out to search for the missing plane, but it was actually a private industry plane that first spotted the wreckage.

Captain Ray Jennings, piloting a trans-Atlantic passenger flight from New York to Cairo spotted the downed Skymaster and advised Gander control that there were survivors in the area.

Two hunters from central Newfoundland, Shea and Gillingham, were the first to arrive at the site and offer assistance to the 18 survivors who had all been injured and burned. Among the survivors were John King, son of the Chinese ambassador to Belgium, and two children of the general manager of the Belgian airline, Gilbert Perrier. Perrier's wife and a third child had been killed in the accident.

Perrier rushed over from Europe, and four helicopters were imported from New York and assembled at Gander. They were used to bring the survivors to a lake five miles from the crash site,

6

where a United States seaplane waited to take them to the Banting Memorial Hospital at Gander.

Rescue parties then cleared an area which was used as a cemetery. Authorities felt it would present too great a risk to attempt to bring the bodies out.

At the completion of the in-air funeral services, bunches of Newfoundland wild flowers were dropped on the graves by relatives of the victims. A monument to those who died in the crash stands at the site, which today is accessible by car.

Louise Journeaux

Louisa Journeaux disappeared on April 18, 1866 from the Island of Jersey near England. Jules Farne was arrested and charged in court with having caused the death or disappearance of the girl, but he was released by the Court because of insufficient evidence. Less that a month later the answer to the Journeaux mystery turned up at St. George's, Newfoundland.

The mystery began on the evening of Louisa's disappearance when she had gone for a boat ride with Farne. A couple who had gone with them in a separate row-boat returned to Jersey to report they had heard calls for help from the Farne boat. When a rescue party searched for the missing pair they found Farne, clinging to a chain at the pierhead, but the girl and the boat had disappeared.

Upon being rescued, Farne claimed they had lost the oars of the boat and that he had jumped in to retrieve them. Both oars were carried away with the tide and Farne decided to swim to shore for help.

An immediate search failed to turn up anything and was called off at midnight. Early the next morning, it was resumed and went on all day. When the party returned empty-handed, Farne was arrested. Although he was released because of insufficient evidence, the people of Jersey believed Farne had killed the girl. Farne fled to Paris because of the growing hostility towards him. As the days passed and there was no sign of what had happened to the girl, her family and friends became convinced she was dead.

Then, on May 10, 1866 a telegraph was received by the missing girl's parents from the Colonial Secretary in Newfoundland. The message caused much excitement throughout Jersey and lifted the spirits of the girl's family and friends. It read: 'Daughter Louisa picked up near England and landed at St. George's Bay. Quite well.'

Farne had told the truth. Their little craft drifted all night and the following morning until it crossed the path of a French ship heading for St. Pierre. The girl was taken on board, treated well, and dropped off safely at St. George's, Newfoundland.

When reports of the bizarre mystery and its conclusion spread around the world, Louisa Journeaux became a celebrity. She was taken to St. John's, dined with the Governor at Government House, and given a complete outfit of clothing by Bowring Brothers' store. When she returned home on June 12, almost two months after she disappeared, a very large crowd turned up to cheer and wish her well.

The Meteorite

The recent report of meteors crashing to earth in the central Newfoundland area brought to mind a similar story. To date, scientists from MUN have searched the areas where the sightings were reported, but have not found any evidence of meteorites. While the story I am about to tell concerns a meteor which actually crashed in Greenland, it does have a connection with Newfoundland. It was a Newfoundland ship, officers, and crew that played a major part in the recovery of the 36.5 ton meteorite.

This huge meteorite was recovered at Cape York, Greenland, near the end of the 19th century and turned over to the American Museum of Natural History. It was Commander Robert Peary of North Pole fame who brought attention of American scientists to the existence of the meteorite. The Americans financed an expedition led by Peary, who chartered a ship from Baine Johnston and Company in St. John's. The Newfoundland firm selected the sealer *Hope*, with Captain John Bartlett of Brigus in command. Bartlett, father of the famous arctic explorer, Bob Bartlett, picked an all Newfoundland crew for the adventure.

On June 5, 1896 the *Hope* sailed out of St. John's for a place called the Devil's Thumb at Hudson Bay, where it picked up three

American scientists from Cornell University in New York. By August 5, the Newfoundland ship reached her Greenland destination. Peary was led to the meteorite by some Greenland eskimos who had visited the site two years earlier. The meteorite, eleven feet in depth and seven in width, was imbedded in the side of a mountain close to the polar icecap. The group found it necessary to use powerful jack screws to lift it. The men then constructed a road half a mile long connecting the site to the harbour where the *Hope* was moored.

It took ten days to move the meteorite from its resting place to the vessel. The Newfoundland crewmembers devised a plan to move the meteorite on board ship. To do this they used heavy timber and large chain tackles attached to winches.

The Newfoundland crew then delivered the scientific find to New York, where it was taken over by the American Museum of Natural History.

The *Hope* was crushed by ice at the seal hunt in 1901, after it had taken 5,000 sealpelts on board.

The Devil Ship

The legend of the mysterious Devil Ship that once visited ports throughout Newfoundland and Labrador was still alive in the Harbour Grace area as late as the 1950s and there may be some people in that area who can still tell the chilling tales of the Black Devil. *The Devil* was an all-black cargo ship with the devil's figure carved on the front. When it landed in port, children stayed away from it and even adults would avoid the wharves after dark. The vessel was believed to be under the control of Satan himself.

As with most legends, this one developed from some true happenings during the late nineteenth century. Originally, the ship was one of two left by a wealthy Englishmen to his two sons. The sons got into a heated argument over the name and finally the older one said, "You may call it the Devil if you wish!"

"The Devil it shall be," the second son replied.

A full-sized figure of Satan was ordered and placed at the front of the ship. The entire ship was painted black and the word 'DEVIL' in large gilded letters was painted at several positions on the ship. It was so ominous to see the black ship with Satan's statue sail into port that the story of the Devil Ship quickly spread.

It was chartered by John Munn and Co. of Harbour Grace in 1875. The company could not keep a steady crew. Each captain and crew drank heavily and attacked each other with whatever weapons could be found.

Even the elements rebelled against the Satanic envoy. Once, during a southwest breeze she dragged her anchor and kept battering Godden's wharf at St. John's. Serious damage resulted to the stern and quarterdeck. When she was repaired, the local police put the captain and the crew on board and ordered them out of port.

When *The Devil* completed a trip from Labrador to England in just six days and eight hours, an outstanding record at the time, the legend of the Devil Ship was enhanced. Suspicion gripped the public to the extent that the British Court of Admiralty ordered the owners to change its name. The name was changed to the *Newsboy*.

While on a trip to the Mediterranean, the bad luck ship was caught in a storm and sunk. It was replaced by its sister ship, the *Sheiton*, the Chinese name for 'Mother of the Devil'.

Monuments and Graves

Some interesting and sometimes amazing circumstances surround many of our famous monuments and cemeteries throughout Newfoundland. For example, perhaps the most amazing burial site in all Canada is the one at the summit of Teahouse Hill, overlooking St. Anthony. The large boulder at the summit is actually the resting place of some famous Newfoundlanders. Interred inside that boulder are the remains of Sir Wilfred Grenfell and his wife, and doctors Charles Curtis and John Little.

Two famous Newfoundland monuments erected as tributes to the Newfoundland Regiment and those who died in both world wars are actually replicas of original ones on display in England and at Beaumont Hamel in France. I am referring to the Fighting Newfoundlander and Caribou monuments. The model for the

Fighting Newfoundlander was Corporal Thomas Pittman. Pittman was thirty years old and stationed at Winchester, England in 1918 when he received a request from a nearby Arts school to go there in full battle gear.

Pittman had already been wounded four times and decorated twice when the invitation to model came. On the day he arrived at the school, armed with gasmask, hand-grenade, and rifle, sculptor Basil Cotto looked him over and said, "All right, you'll do." Pittman posed for one hour every day for two months for the famous bronze statue depicting an infantryman preparing to throw a grenade in battle. The replica of that statue was donated to the city of St. John's by Edgar Bowring.

In 1928, another tribute to the Regiment was erected at Bowring Park. It was a replica of the Caribou on display at Beaumont Hamel Park, France, where hundreds of Newfoundlanders are buried. Another monument, known as the Sergeant's War Memorial, at Queen's Road and Cathedral Street in St. John's, was unveiled in 1921. It was constructed by the Sergeant's Mess of the Royal Newfoundland Regiment, in memory of non-commissioned officers who died in World War I.

There is a fourteen foot monument on Cavendish Square, opposite Hotel Newfoundland which hundreds pass every day and may not know for whom it was dedicated. The monument was erected in memory of a Newfoundland nurse, Ethel Dickenson, who lost her life while fighting a serious influenza epidemic that swept St. John's during August 1918. The inscription reads, 'She gave her life while tending patients at the King George V Institute, St. John's.'

Finally, one memorial, which, if authorized, would be the greatest memorial of all time, is the five-foot-high boulder just twenty yards from the sea at Grate's Cove, Trinity Bay. Carved in the boulder is the Italian name of John Cabot, 'I. Caboto' and those of his crewmembers. Leo English, a former Newfoundland archivist, believed it was authentic, but there is no way of ascertaining the date of the inscription, or of authenticating it.

A Spectacular Sky Show

In 1936 Newfoundlanders were baffled by the appearance in the skies of great balls of fire with smoke trailing behind them as they headed for earth. These sightings were not confined to one area and could be seen all over the Island. The actual date of this strange phenomenon was October 19, 1936 and reports of the sightings poured into St. John's from all over Newfoundland.

The whole spectacle lasted fifteen minutes and occurred between 2:45 and 3 p.m. in broad daylight on a Monday afternoon. A sampling of some of the telegraphs received indicates the extent of the phenomena.

One from Conception Harbour reads: "Saw something fall from the sky which seemed to be eighteen feet long. When it fell, smoke appeared to rise from it. It appeared to fall at a place called Dock Bridge near Avondale."

A message from Merasheen read, "An object which burst into flames emitting a cloud of smoke dropped apparently 20 miles northwest of here."

And a telegraph from St. Jacques stated, "A strange phenomenon was seen in the sky here resembling a ball of fire followed shortly by a sound of an explosion and what appeared to be smoke followed the explosion."

From New Harbour came another telegraph stating, "What happened to be a ball of fire fell from the sky northwest of here. It was followed by a long trail of smoke."

At Port Blandford, a witness reported, "A ball of fire was seen to fall from miles west of here and was followed by an explosion and a lot of dark smoke."

A telegram from Old Perlican described a similar sighting: A flaming meteor about ten feet long fell in the water about three miles northwest of here. It was followed by a stream of smoke."

Another telegram from Burnt Island reported a large flame seen heading towards earth which upon impact made a loud explosion.

Harbour Main, Great Harbour, and Rancontre East all reported sighting large fireballs and streaming smoke falling to earth. The one at Harbour Main differed from the others because it was a shining bright silver colour.

The sightings caused all sorts of speculation, but the official explanation given for this strange phenomenon was that Newfoundland had passed through the strange astronomical event known as a 'shower of meteors'.

Giant Squid

When famous U. S. author Charles Berlitz wrote his book *Bermuda Triangle* in the early 1970s, he speculated that giant squid existed, but that there was no actual proof of their existence. When I first read Berlitz's book I was vacationing at Florida and I contacted him with information proving that the giant squid did indeed exist. I recalled that I once attended a press conference at the Marine Science Lab, Logy Bay, in which Dr. Fred Aldrich, world authority on the giant squid, confirmed that the Lab had in its possession one of these sea monsters.

In addition to Dr. Aldrich's work; scientific records, apparently long-forgotten, also prove the monster's existence in Newfoundland as early as October 26, 1873. On that day, Theophilius Piccott, Dan Squires, and Piccott's 12-year-old son Tom, were fishing off the Bell Island coast when they saw a strange object floating on the water's surface. The trio rowed closer to have a look and one of the men struck it with an oar. Suddenly, the object came to life and rose up out of the water. Its large eyes and long tentacles frightened the men and the young boy. The sea monster moved closer and began wrapping its tentacles around the dory, dragging it into the sea. The young boy grabbed his hatchet and began chopping off the monster's tentacles. The squid fell back into the waters and, as it did, it ejected a quantity of inky fluid which darkened the waters. The men estimated that the tentacles of the squid were more than ten feet long, and the body about six feet long. It was about five feet in diameter and looked very much like a large squid.

The fishermen rowed back to shore carrying with them the two tentacles as proof that the giant squid did exist. The shorter tentacle was given to dogs to eat, while the longer one was sent to St. John's to Reverend Moses Harvey, who was known at the time as a knowledgeable naturalist and someone who might value the object. Harvey wrote to a friend, "I am now in possession of one of the rarest curiosities in the whole animal kingdom, the veritable arm of the devil fish, about whose existence naturalists have been disputing for centuries. I know that I hold in my hand the key to the great mystery."

An article written by Harvey on the subject along with pictures was published in the Natural History Society of England's national magazine. He also sent some of the suckers which he cut from its arm. The story attracted world-wide attention, but as the years passed and no further proof came forward, Harvey's discovery was forgotten.

Giant squids taken from Newfoundland waters are brought to the Marine Sciences Lab at Marine Drive near St. John's to be studied by experts.
Photo — Jack Fitzgerald

Two Amazing Stories

Two unusual stories, although not related, are perhaps among the most intriguing of the many such stories from our colourful past. The first deals with one of the most amazing events ever to occur at sea. It took place on a ship sailing from Bristol to Newfoundland. The name of the vessel was the *Tuscanny*. It was under the command of Captain Edward Power, and carried passengers and fishermen heading for Newfoundland. While only one day at sea, the *Tuscanny* encountered the French Duke de Biron's *Privateer*, which immediately opened fire on them. The *Tuscanny* was carrying a cargo of explosives, and, when the *Privateer*'s shots hit it, the vessel blew up. Out of the 211 people on board, only the Captain and four others were saved. Among the survivors was an infant.

The infant was saved in a most unusual way. When the explosion occurred, the infant was blown completely away from the *Tuscanny* and landed unhurt on the deck of the French ship. This story is recorded in the Annual Register of Great Britain and happened in 1761. It is described in the register as the most amazing and unusual situation ever to occur at sea.

* * *

The second story deals with the giveaway of a fortune by a man who was unaware of its true value. A treasure-piece worth in excess of $100,000 was in the possession of Sean O'Brien, a great grandfather of the late John O'Brien of St. John's. But because O'Brien was unable to assess the true value of the object, he willingly accepted $25.00 for it from a County Kerry jeweller.

The item was a solid gold eighteen-inch altar piece which was given by Mary Queen of Scots to a Jesuit priest on the eve of her execution. After poor O'Brien sold the piece to the jeweller, that same jeweller thought he was getting a bargain when he resold the item to a County Cork jeweller for $35.00. The County Cork jeweller then made another profit by selling it to a Dublin antique dealer for $45.00.

The antique dealer researched the history of the item and discovered its true identity. He then sold it to an American millionaire for $103,000.

The O'Briens of County Kerry and St. John's lost possession of an item that at today's value would be worth in excess of $300,000.

Curious Event

A curious event took place in the narrows of St. John's Harbour during the summer of 1848. Eighteen-year-old Kenneth McLea, son of one of the partners in the fish-exporting firm of J. and W. Steward, decided to go sailing around the harbour on July 19th.

He invited two workers from his father's firm to join him. They were T. P. Hall and Alex McKenzie. As they neared the narrows, a sudden squall came up, causing their small vessel to overturn. The men hung on as the boat tossed around, but all three disappeared beneath the water.

The accident was seen from the *H.M.S. Alarm*, which was docked nearby. The captain dispatched a rescue boat immediately. McKenzie was pulled from the water but Hall and young McLea had disappeared. A group of small boats from around St. John's searched for the bodies that afternoon and into the next day. They recovered Hall, but could find no trace of McLea.

The assistance of the Royal Artillery was requested, and that group moved a large six-pounder cannon aboard a small craft and sailed to the accident site.

The gunmen fired a succession of rounds of gunfire. Each blast caused the boat to swing around. When the cannon fire was completed, dragging resumed, and the body of Ken McLea was easily recovered. The body had apparently become stuck in mud or weeds and the cannon blasting shook it loose.

This seems to have been the only case on record of the use of blasting cannons to recover the body of a drowning victim in Newfoundland.

A West Coast Mystery

On the evening of March 15, 1909 Frank Penny discovered the body of a man in a wooded area near the Humber River Pulp and Lumber Company near Deer Lake. The police were called to the scene and the man was identified as a Frenchman named Millere. When the police searched the dead man's clothing they found some very surprising and mysterious material.

Millere's pockets were filled with every conceivable type of drawing of an astronomical nature and plans and sketches of the design and building of aircraft.

Along with the drawings, the police found writings which were highly imaginative descriptions of the planets and crazy philosophical dissertations on the relationship between humanity and the heavenly bodies. The most intriguing and amazing of all the evidence was a post office receipt issued at Summerside, Prince Edward Island, showing that Jacques E, Millere had recently sent a registered letter to the Duke of Orleans in Paris.

Who was this Millere? One newspaper suggested that he might have been some visionary royalist dreaming of the restoration of the French monarchy or some science-obsessed crackpot. Another paper observed that Millere may have been carrying out research in the field of astrology. The paper claimed that there was no mystery to it at all. Whatever the Frenchman was up to the mystery was never solved, and for all we know, there may have been a story as fantastic as any which the great Jules Vernes wrote.

Jacques Millere was buried at the Catholic Cemetery at Birchy Cove. His connection with the Duke of Orleans also remains a mystery.

A Perilous Feat

Former Premier and historian Joey Smallwood, described the amazing feat of Captain George Barbour and his crew in making emergency repairs to the sealing vessel *Nascopi* at the ice fields in 1912 as one of the most extraordinary and perilous feats ever performed on the sea.

The crisis arose when three blades of the *Nascopi* smashed in the ice, leaving the vessel stranded between the Funks and the Straits of Belle Isle. Smallwood said, "It is more likely that anyone but a Newfoundland sealing captain would have abandoned the seal hunt then and there and wired for a rescue ship, but Newfoundlanders have always been noted for their ingenuity and determination and Captain Barbour determined to see what could be done."

He discussed with his engineers the possibility of putting a reserve propeller on her without going back to port. The engineers felt it could be done if they could get the steamer's stern high enough out of the water. But this would present another problem. With the stern raised, the bow would be well down in the water. Captain Barbour felt the problem could be overcome if they could get the right balance, thereby preventing a nosedive.

The *Nascopi*, a large steamer carrying a crew of 270, was owned by Job Brothers and Company. Barbour and his crew were a resourceful and courageous lot; they set out to perform the very dangerous manoeuvre. Smallwood described the deed as 'one of the most desperately hazardous feats ever accomplished on the sea'. The crew was divided into four watches with each watch working three hours at a stretch. They shifted the cargo of coal from the aft part of the steamer to the forward part.

Every moment was a tortuous one as the stern began to lengthen and rise and the stem began to drop more and more. Every ton taken from aft to forward was lifting the stern higher, but it was settling her deeper and deeper. Added to this danger was the possibility of a sudden windstorm springing up which would have certainly sent the vessel to the bottom.

As soon as the stern was high enough out of the water, the

engineers went to work with hammers and wrenches, working feverishly to get the new blades safely and securely adjusted. When the work was finished, all 270 men cheered loudly. The undertaking was successful and the *Nascopi* that year took 17,057 seal pelts, the second-heaviest load for the season.

A Mystery Find at Bay Bulls

If public suspicions concerning the recovery of an ancient mysterious object from the harbour at Bay Bulls on September 23, 1943 had been confirmed, it would have disproven a contemporary version of a major historical event in Newfoundland history. During World War Two, the Royal Canadian Navy operated a repair and supply base at Bay Bulls. While the Bay Bulls harbour was being dredged to accommodate the navy, a strange and curious object was brought up from the bottom. Dredging was being carried out by the Cape Shore Construction Company. One of its steam-shovels picked up a piece of metal that caused excitement throughout Newfoundland.

The engineer on the job, a man named Jenkins, reported that the object had been found in about four feet of silt, fifty feet from the shore. It was made of lead and measured eighteen inches long, four inches wide and two inches deep. It was a hollow, oblong object which may at one time have been affixed to a post. It had been flattened on both ends and seemed to have been hacked by some rough implement.

A crest or seal was soldered into the piping. On one side appeared to be the copy of a seal in oval form with a face in bold relief surrounded by a scroll of possibly flowers or leaves. There was no lettering in the object but a series of undecipherable numbers appeared on top.

On September 24, Dr. Vincent Burke, president of the Newfoundland Historical Society, and members of the press went to Bay Bulls to inspect the discovery. There was some public speculation that it was the Royal Arms used by Sir Humphery Gilbert to claim Newfoundland for England in 1583. Gilbert had the Royal Arms, cut in lead and affixed to a pillar which he put into the earth when he made his historic claim.

Harvey's's *History of Newfoundland* describing the event stated, 'The banner of England was hoisted on a flagstaff, the Royal Arms, cut in lead, was affixed to a pillar near the water's edge to mark the ceremony.'

If the discovered object was Sir Humphrey Gilbert's, the question arises as to how it got into Bay Bulls Harbour. Could Gilbert have mistakenly sailed into Bay Bulls thinking it was St. John's?

The mystery object was turned over to the Hon. H. A. Winter, Commissioner for Home Affairs and Education for Newfoundland, who sent it to the College of Heralds in London for examination and identification. The object was declared to have no historic value and since that time, its whereabouts have been unknown.

Chapter II
WE CAN BE PROUD
OF THESE NEWFOUNDLANDERS

There is hardly a field of endeavour in which a Newfoundlander has not excelled. Some of the stories I have gathered of such Newfoundlanders include those who gained recognition in journalism, medicine, sport, writing, exploration, entertainment; one who made *Ripley's Believe It or Not* and another who was close to the King of France.

The Mysterious Letter from France

In 1847, Reverend M. Chapman of Fogo received a mysterious letter which lead, some years later, to the revelation of a connection between Nancy Simms of Fogo, the Royal Family of France, and a great Irish patriot, Sir Edward Fitzgerald. The letter was written in French and neither the Reverend nor anyone else in the community could read it. Years later, when finally translated, it led to one of the most dramatic, romantic, and tragic stories in our history.

The letter was written by King Louis Phillippe of France, who was seeking information on the Simms family of Fogo; and particularly Pamela Simms. The reason for the king's interest in the girl from Fogo was even more startling than finding out who had written the letter. Pamela was the stepsister of King Louis XIV, and had lived with the king's family from the time she was five.

Pamela had been born at Fogo out of wedlock in 1770 to Jeremiah Coughlan and a girl named Nancy Simms. At the age of five Coughlan took her, along with her mother, to London, where he planned to marry Nancy. Once in London, however, Coughlan deserted his family. Faced with poverty, Nancy Simms gave up her child to a wealthy French family who had been seeking a companion for their own small children. The family was that of the Duke of Orleans. Pamela's stepbrother was destined to become King of France. The family was so fond of Pamela that, while they were in exile in London and themselves a mere step above poverty, they would often take the blankets from their own children, during winter frosts, to cover little Pamela, because she seemed weaker than the others. There is a valuable painting in the Palace of Versailles depicting King Louis' sister and Madame Gelanas, who cared for the royal children; each playing a harp while Pamela held the music sheets for them. Pamela grew up to become one of the most beautiful women in Europe and, after several courtships with prominent Europeans, she married the Irish patriot, Sir Edward Fitzgerald. Louis was a witness at the wedding.

When the British learned that Sir Edward was secretly plotting an alliance between Ireland and France against the English, Sir Edward was arrested. He was mortally wounded during the arrest and although he survived for a day after, and pleaded to have his wife brought to his side, the British refused.

After Sir Edward's death, Pamela went to Hamburg and lived there with Madame Gelanas. From there she entered a convent. In 1830 Louis became King Louis Phillippe of France. A year later, Pamela passed away. Prince Tallyrand represented the King at funeral services, and King Louis Phillippe and Princess Adelaide made a special visit to the grave of the lady from Fogo, who had once had been a part of their family.

A Great Journalist

Two news-stories, among the greatest in world history, were written by a Newfoundlander. John Mitchell was born at St. John's on September 21, 1853 and educated at St. Bonaventure's College. He later wrote these stories for the famous New York Herald.

When he graduated from St. Bon's, he went to work at the Anglo-American Cable Company, Heart's Content. He quickly became an expert telegraph operator and had no trouble getting a job with the New York Herald on its telegraph staff. He achieved a reputation as the top telegraph operator in the United States and was promoted to night-manager of the Herald.

When the Spanish-American War broke out in 1898, Mitchell was sent to Kingston, Jamaica to cover the war by telegraph. The war was receiving world-wide attention and the two biggest stories to come out of the conflict were of the battle at Santiago and the wiping out of the Spanish Fleet.

In just three days, Mitchell had sent 5,000 words at a cost of one dollar per word. As a result of his work, the New York Herald had a world-newspaper exclusive on American successes in the Spanish-American War.

John Mitchell is also known for his part in the transmission to New York of the first wireless message flashed from incoming Atlantic steamships.

Mitchell was placed in charge of a company of telegraph operators sent by the New York Herald in 1901 to Nantucket to demonstrate wireless communications to and from ships. This was the first practical demonstration of its kind.

John Mitchell passed away in 1908 and was buried at Brooklyn, New York.

Mitchell was educated at St. Bonaventure's College, St. John's and went on to a successful career as a journalist in the United States.

Photo — Jack Fitzgerald

Sir Thomas Roddick

Newfoundland history is filled with stories of native-born Newfoundlanders venturing out all over the world and gaining fame and recognition for their achievements. On July 31, 1846 one such Newfoundlander, who became a giant in Canadian medical history, was born at Harbour Grace. He was Thomas Roddick, son of John Roddick, principal of the Harbour Grace Grammar School. Over the next fifty years, young Roddick was to become one of the most outstanding doctors in the British Empire and would earn fame and recognition for his contribution to the medical profession in this country.

Thomas Roddick became a doctor and was quickly seen as a promising and brilliant young medical man. He was the first chief surgeon of the Royal Victoria Hospital, Montreal, and became a dynamic force in Canadian medicine. During the 1870s, after spending some time in Edinburgh, Scotland with the renowned Dr. Lister, Roddick returned to Canada and championed the cause of Lister's antiseptic methods, a new and radical idea at that time.

His greatest accomplishment in medicine was his founding of the Canadian Medical Council, which assured uniform standards of medical education in all the provinces. He became the Council's first president. In 1896 he was elected to parliament and championed some of the causes put forward by the Medical Council.

Before moving permanently to mainland Canada, Dr. Roddick worked at McMurdo's Drug Store in St. John's and was a partner with Dr. Charles Renouf. Roddick once assisted Renouf in removing a man's lower jaw without benefit of an anesthetic.

Roddick had a thirst for adventure and was involved with the Canadian military in putting down the Finian Rebellion. In 1885 he became the first Canadian director of medical services in a military campaign. That campaign was the suppression of the Reil Rebellion. Reil was arrested and was medically treated by Dr. Roddick. The rebel leader wrote a note and signed his autograph in the doctor's notebook. Roddick made every effort to save Reil's life on medical grounds, but without success: Reil was executed.

In 1897, for the first time in the history of the British Empire, the British Medical Society honoured a doctor outside the British Isles: that man was Dr. Thomas Roddick.

In 1914 Thomas Roddick became Sir Thomas Roddick, being knighted by King George V in recognition of his service to medicine and mankind.

Roddickton, at White Bay, is called after our famous son, and a hospital at Stephenville was also named, in his honour, the *Sir Thomas Roddick Hospital*.

Newfoundlander U. S. Boxing Champ

A Newfoundlander, the boxing champion of all America! Unbelievable, but true! Not only did he win the title, but after winning the twelve round fight for the honour of the title *American Boxing Champion*, he never fought again!

In 1879 Joe Goss held the American title but had not defended it for three years. That year, Jimmy Elliott, who had been featherweight champion of America when he was only 16, was released from prison, where he had served some years for robbery. He challenged Goss for the title.

Goss was then 34 and not too interested in fighting. He refused Elliott's challenge and Elliott claimed the title. Then, to sanction Elliott as the new American Champion, promoters sought a suitable opponent for him to fight for the title.

Johnny Dwyer, who had been born in a house near the Cross Roads on Water Street West on August 15, 1845, was the same age as Elliot and had a big reputation around New York as a fearless and successful fighter. He had moved to Brooklyn when his family emigrated to the U. S. some years earlier and had settled down in Irishtown. He was a regular fighter at the popular gym at Houston and Crosby Streets in New York which was operated by fight promoter Henry Hill.

George Law, an eccentric millionaire, took an interest in young Dwyer and financed his training. In several exhibition bouts Dwyer defeated former champs Joe Coburn and Tom Allen. Boxing promoters felt that Dwyer would be an excellent opponent for 'Greyback Elliott', as he was called. Johnny was reluctant, as it would be his first bare-knuckled fight under the London prize ring rules, while Elliott was a veteran of many such fights.

The fight was held at Long Point, Ontario. Elliott seemed to have the edge in height, weight, and reach. In the first round, Dwyer gave Elliott a hard blow over the temple, which weakened him for subsequent rounds.

By the seventh round, Elliott was taking a beating. In desperation he tried to gouge Dwyer's eyes, using turpentine on his thumbs. He followed this by kicking Dwyer to the floor. The seconds used water to clean Dwyer's eyes and the fight resumed. Instead of weakening Dwyer, Elliott had made him more determined to win. Dwyer went on to pound Elliott in each round, finally knocking him unconscious in the 12th and being crowned American Boxing Champion.

Dwyer refused to fight again. Paddy Ryan, the man promoters scheduled to fight Dwyer, went on to fight Joe Goss, beating him in a record 87 rounds; but was himself defeated for the title by John L. Sullivan.

A recent photo of Water Street West in St. John's where U.S. Boxing Champ Johnny Dwyer once lived.

Photo — Jack Fitzgerald

The Golden Fleece

The famous book, *The Golden Fleece*, was written by Sir William Vaughan. Vaughan, the author of twelve books, also had a close connection with Newfoundland.

Sir William Vaughan was born in 1577 and died in 1641. He entered Oxford University at the age of fourteen, and finished his education at the age of 28, having earned a Master of Arts degree.

Sir William lived for three years at Fermeuse, which is shown on John Mason's ancient map as a community then called Golden Grove. While in Newfoundland, Vaughan wrote two books. One was called *Newfoundland Cures*; only one copy of which is now in existence, and that is at the British Museum in London. The second was his best known book, *The Golden Fleece*. Vaughan had stated that the true Golden Fleece was to be found in Newfoundland. He had nothing but praise for all that he found there, including the weather.

Vaughan brought a group of people to Newfoundland to colonize the Ferryland area. However this was a drain on his resources and he had to sell a strip of land at Placentia Bay about six miles in length. He sold more of his land to Lord Baltimore.

Vaughan's colonists were poorly chosen. Even Richard Whitbourne had to resign the governorship because he could do nothing with them. Vaughan's colony was founded in 1617 and at first was called 'Cambriol Colchis', which later became known as Trepassey.

Vaughan's books helped Newfoundland colonization and some of the descendants of his colonists have been amongst the best of all Newfoundland settlers.

Clinch — First Vaccine

Reverend John Clinch was a medical doctor as well as a clergyman. He practiced medicine at Trinity and Bonavista Bay; and married Hannah Hart of English Harbour and had five children: four sons and one daughter. While Clinch earned his place in the history of Trinity through his thirty years of service as priest and doctor, he is best remembered and most widely known for his connection with vaccination in Newfoundland.

It was Dr. Clinch who administered for the first time in North America the smallpox vaccine which had just been discovered by Dr. Edward Jenner of London. The vaccine was sent personally to Dr. Clinch by its inventor because the two were intimate friends, having studied together at the London Medical College.

After Clinch came to Newfoundland, the two kept in touch with each other. When Clinch complained to Jenner of catarrhal trouble, Jenner wrote him saying: 'If that matter should dare to molest you next year, retreat, seek the milder shores of old England and leave the land of snow and ice to the bears for whom it was made.'

Jenner was aware of the smallpox problems in Newfoundland and he wasted no time in sending the vaccine to his old friend. It was delivered by Jenner's nephew, Reverend George Jenner, who became Church of England minister at Harbour Grace. Clinch first tried the vaccine on himself and children. He then inoculated 700 people of all ages. The vaccination was a true miracle.

Clinch passed away at Trinity on November 22, 1819 and was buried beneath the altar of the Anglican Church there. When that church was torn down, his grave was left in the open churchyard where it can be seen today.

Alex Macay

A man who played a principle part in world tele-communications was the father of electricity in Newfoundland. Alexander Macay, was born at Pictou, Nova Scotia, and adopted Newfoundland as his permanent home. He was a friend and employee of world-famous Cyrus Field. Field had enough faith in Macay to put him in charge of his operation in New York, London, and Newfoundland.

When the Great Eastern landed the first trans-Atlantic cable at Heart's Content, the enthusiastic Macay walked into the water to bring the cable ashore.

Macay was brought to Newfoundland by Cyrus Field to prepare for the trans-Atlantic cable operation. He was a stickler for detail and once walked every inch of a telegraph line from Cape Race to Cape Ray to satisfy himself that all construction details had been carried out.

While visiting Montreal, Macay saw an electric lightbulb in operation for the first time. He immediately envisioned introducing the new invention to Newfoundland. After he discussed this proposal with the Royal Electric Company of Montreal, he returned to Newfoundland to form the St. John's Light Company. He raised the $32,000 capital for the venture in just three days and became the first president of the company, which was a forerunner of the Newfoundland Light and Power Company. Electric lights were first used in Newfoundland by the new company on October 17, 1885.

Macay earned a place in history by also introducing the first public telephone system to Newfoundland. He operated a telephone exchange on Water Street for city businessmen. That building was destroyed in the Great Fire of 1892 but the exchange was reopened later in a building on New Gower Street.

Alexander Macay developed a deep pride and love for his adopted home in Newfoundland. The high regard and respect by the people of Newfoundland for Macay was evidenced by his continual election to the Newfoundland legislature for twenty-two years.

Captain Victor Campbell

Captain Victor Campbell, who settled at Black Duck, Newfoundland, during the early 1920s, and later moved to Corner Brook, was a senior officer with the tragic Scott Polar Expedition in 1912, — and one of the heroes of the event. Scott's dash to the South Pole was made during 1912, but he was beaten to it by a Norwegian expedition under Roald Amundsen. Scott's group perished during their return. Scott's support-group was made up of several units, and Campbell was leader of one of these units.

The vessel used for the expedition, the *Terra Nova*, was a Newfoundland sealing vessel owned by Bowring Brothers. The *Terra Nova* dropped Campbell's unit near Cape Adare, just north of the Ross Barrier, during February 1911. The group was assigned to carry out geological work until the steamer came back for them. Campbell later moved his group to Victoria Land, closer to the main base and the South Pole.

A winter of unbelievable hardships and danger was forced upon Campbell and his men when the *Terra Nova* became caught in ice and was unable to return to pick them up at the scheduled time, two months later. Faced with the reality of being stranded for a severe polar winter, Campbell began immediate preparations for the ordeal. To start with, the tent was not strong enough to withstand the winter gales, so Campbell and his men cut an igloo-type cave in the ice and began stocking up on food. They caught nine seals, and 118 penguins. This food supply had to be replenished again before their ordeal was over.

The igloo was 13 feet long, nine feet wide, and not high enough for a person to stand. All the men came down with a condition known as 'igloo back', cause by being forced to stoop for several months. Their clothes were wet and soiled from carrying blubber. To break the monotony of the diet during the long winter, they occasionally ate plant life found in the stomach of the seals. Their main dish was *hoosh*, a combination of seal and penguin topped off with biscuit and a cup of cocoa. All the men came down with a form of dysentry, creating a new danger. Having to leave the igloo brought with it the strong possibility of frostbite. To deal with this, a small latrine was made near the entrance to the cave.

They used blubber to fuel their stove, which was an oil can cut down. Several smaller tins were also cut down, filled with melted blubber, and, with a strand of rope for a wick, were used as lanterns. Campbell made use of a small library to keep up morale. Men were assigned lectures to prepare, which they each delivered in turn. Church services were held on Sundays.

By the time the *Terra Nova* got through, Campbell's men had moved on to another support-base, from which they were eventually rescued. When Scott's brother-in-law, Captain Bruce, read the diary of Campbell, he cried.

Captain Victor Campbell chose Newfoundland as his home and died at Corner Brook during November, 1956 at the age of 82. He was given a full military burial by the Corner Brook Branch of the Royal Canadian Legion.

Captain Bob Bartlett

Captain Bob Bartlett was born at Brigus on August 15, 1875. He was one of Newfoundland's most outstanding sea-captains, and once toured the world lecturing on his experiences in the Arctic and near the North Pole. Bartlett's interest in the sea started at an early age, and while still in his early teens he went to the seal fishery. At nineteen he became master of a schooner and by twenty-two he had gotten his first taste of polar exploration.

That same year he signed on as mate on the *Windward*, owned by Admiral Peary, and under the command of his uncle, Captain John Bartlett. On his first trip north, the *Windward* spent the winter at Hudson's Bay.

Bartlett, as a child, was delicate and sickly, and a sea career for him seemed out of the question. He attended Methodist College in St. John's, but his attraction to ships and the sea was beginning to take root. Young Bob would frequently 'pip off' from school only to be found later at the St. John's Waterfront, watching ships coming and going. Eventually he went on to write his master's exams at the Nautical Academy at Halifax.

Admiral Peary was so impressed by the abilities of the young Newfoundlander that he gave Bartlett command of the *Roosevelt*.

Bartlett was only twenty-eight years old at the time. Peary was preparing him for his role in Peary's expedition to the North Pole. Bartlett accepted the post on the condition that, when he had worked the ship as far north as possible, he would be allowed to accompany Peary on the final dash to the Pole.

Peary assigned Bartlett command of a party which set out to reach the 88th parallel. He brought his group to within twenty miles of the Pole, at which time, due to the weather, Peary ordered him back to keep open the line of communications. Admiral Peary wrote in his logbook that 'Bartlett had done good work and had been a great help to me. I have given him this post of honour because he was fit for it.'

When Peary made his final dash to the Pole, Bartlett was not chosen to go with him. American author John Edward Weens, in his book published in 1967, dealing with the world-famous Admiral Peary, suggested that Peary had sent Bartlett back because he wanted it to be an all-American project.

Bartlett however, did not share this view. He wrote in his logbook: 'I do not deny that it would have been a great thrill to have stood at the peak of our globe, and that it would have helped me make money from lectures. But do not forget that Hansen was a better dog-driver than I. So, I think Peary's decision was wise and I have never held it against him.'

The expedition made both Peary and Bartlett famous and they both went on a world-wide tour of lectures. Bartlett also played the part of the ship captain in Varrick Frissell's movie *The Viking*. Frissell was killed when the movie crew returned a year later to add some action scenes and the *Viking* exploded. Bartlett passed away after suffering pneumonia, at a New York hospital in 1946.

This beautiful cottage in a splendid garden setting at Brigus was the home of Captain Bob Bartlett.

Photo — Jack Fitzgerald

Georgina Stirling

Georgina Stirling toured the world opera centres during 1897 and 1898 and is remembered as a prima donna soprano. Georgina, youngest of seven children of Dr. William Stirling, studied music at Paris, Italy, and Germany.

Her stage name was Mademoiselle Toulinquet and she once toured the United States with the famous Colonel M. Apelson's Imperial Opera. The editor of the *Twillingate Sun* at the time described her as a 'very striking woman, a woman of strong opinion, but very sociable, very aristocratic.'

Before entering the world of opera, Georgina was given some advice by Madame de Alberti, a music connoisseur and mother-in-law of Sir Charles Hutton. Madame de Alberti told Georgina that she had a fine voice to sing oratoria and ballad, but certainly not opera. But Georgina was strong-willed and determined to become an opera singer.

She proved Madame de Alberti wrong.

On one of her appearances at Rome, an Italian maestro told her, 'Madame, you have the voice of an angel, but the face of a devil.'

After the turn of the century, Georgina Stirling developed a throat ailment that almost destroyed her voice. She became very depressed and took up heavy drinking in St. John's. This episode in her life did not last long and she returned to Twillingate, where she lived a life of charity and elegance. At Twillingate, Georgina Stirling turned her talents to helping others. She founded the Dorcas Society which made clothing for the poor. She frequently gave concerts in St. John's and Twillingate and gave all proceeds to charity.

Captain Abe Kean

During 1934, Captain Abe Kean was given a hero's welcome upon returning to St. John's from the annual seal hunt. He was honored at a host of banquets and dinners throughout the island;

made a member of the Order of the British Empire; and was mentioned in *Ripley's Believe It or Not*.

The event which made Kean the centre of public attention and admiration was the record established that year when, after forty years going to the seal hunt, he reached the one million mark in seal-killing.

There was a great deal of public interest in Kean's trip to the ice in 1934, because he was just 40,300 short of the million mark. People all over Newfoundland were speculating and betting on his chances of making the record. When Kean was aboard the *Beothuck*, preparing to leave, he received a message form the president of the Newfoundland Board of Trade stating, 'If you reach your million, we will put on the biggest flipper dinner ever given.' Of course Kean was expected to supply the flippers.

On that same day, another message came from a friend at Change Islands stating, 'All Change Islands are praying for you.'

Kean wired back, 'Tell them to pray without ceasing.'

It was on the morning of April 2, 1934 that Captain Abe Kean set his record of killing one million seals. As the record was established, all the 225 crewmembers of Kean's ship gathered on deck and cheered and whistled as the record-breaking seals were piled on deck. Kean's son, Captain W. B. Kean went on radio at 7:00 p.m. to broadcast to all Newfoundland that his father had reached the million mark.

Congratulatory messages began to pour in from all over the island. The first was from John Parker of Parker and Monroe's; others were from Sir John Hope Simpson, Bowring family, and Admiral David Murray Anderson. When the *Beothuck* arrived in the city, crowds turned up with flags to cheer him. Bowring Brothers presented him with a silver medal on a pedestal and the Board of Trade kept their promise and honoured Newfoundland's most famous seal killer with a flipper dinner, at which time they presented him with a model of his ship.

On June 3 that year, the King's birthday, Captain Abe Kean was honoured with the Order of the British Empire in recognition of his success at the ice. Kean had made sealing history.

Kean also had some political success in his life, having been elected twice to the Newfoundland Legislature, and once served as Minister of Marine and Fisheries. He wrote a book entitled *Old and Young Ahead*, which was published in 1935.

Newfoundlander Held
World Sporting Record

Bob Fowlow, born at Trinity Bay in 1882, and later a graduate of St. Bon's College in St. John's, is listed among the world's greatest marathon runners having held the world's outdoor running record. Brother Morris, the running coach at St. Bon's, instilled in Fowlow the needed dedication and desire to excel in the sport of running. Bob moved with his family to Boston in 1898, and joined a sporting organization known as the Crescent Club. One of the club's favourite activities was a three mile running competition against runners from the Cambridge Port Association. The race was usually won by a Portuguese member member of the Cambridge Club. He was such a strong runner that he would give his competitors a minute start before starting himself.

Bob's brother Frank argued with the Portuguese, challenging him to race his brother, and claiming that Bob could easily beat him. The Portuguese became angry and accepted the challenge. Bob however, refused to accept the headstart offered and insisted that both runners start at the same time. There was a great deal of public interest in the race, not just because many wanted to see the Portuguese beaten, but also because Bob challenged him to a fist-fight after the race.

There was some disappointment at first, because the Portuguese took an early lead; but this changed to cheering when Bob caught up and passed his opponent. Bob Fowlow went on to win the race. His reputation as a runner in the Boston area was just beginning to grow. In 1901 he came ninth in the 26 mile Boston Marathon, fourth in the 26 mile marathon at the World's Fair in St. Louis in 1904, and, in 1906 came in the first six runners of several National American running marathons. Because of his strong showing, Bob was selected to represent the United States at the Olympic Games in Athens, Greece. Running in the Olympic Marathon, Bob was holding down third place when he had to stop because of sore feet.

In 1907, Bob was back in good form, and in that year he broke the world's record for the 26 mile run by running the Boston

Marathon in 2 hours 25 minutes. Although he broke the World Record, he did not win that race. He came in second to Indian Tom Longboat, who beat Fowlow by 26 seconds. Fowlow could have won the race, but had to stop at a railway crossing for two and a half minutes to wait for a 45-car freight train to pass by.

In 1909, on New Year's Day, Bob broke the American record in a 26 mile race run at the Empire Track in New York. A week later, he won the World's Outdoor running marathon at Boston and set a new world's record. At the end of that race, he received one of the greatest ovations ever given an athlete in Boston.

Henry Supple

There was a time when the name Henry Supple was a household name throughout Newfoundland. Supple was well known during the mid 19th century as a champion of fishermen's rights. During 1858 he led the famous Sealer's Protest Parade, demanding free berths to the seal fishery.

While Henry Supple Sr. had made a name for himself in this country, his son Henry made a name in the United States, but for quite different reasons. Henry Jr. became known for pulling off one of the greatest publicity stunts of the 19th century.

Henry Jr. had moved to Brooklyn, New York from St. John's after finishing school, and became employed by the Roebling family there as a master mechanic on a project to build the Brooklyn Bridge. The idea for the bridge to cross the East River between Brooklyn and Manhattan was the brainchild of John Roebling, a New York engineer and construction company owner.

Shortly after the project got underway, Roebling died and the work was left to his son Washington to complete. The first strand of steel wire linking the two 278 foot high towers constructed on either side of the East River was connected on August 14, 1876.

To mark the historic occasion, and to focus national attention on the Brooklyn Bridge Project, Washington Roebling worked with young Supple in planning the famous stunt. This stunt involved setting up a bosun's chair on the wire to carry Supple across. The stunt was a dangerous one, as high winds almost forced young Supple out of the chair on several occasions. But the young Newfoundlander had nerves of steel, and, when he successfully arrived on the other side, he was greeted with a great ovation and an army of reporters from all over the United States.

Henry Supple Jr. went on to supervise the construction of the Brooklyn Bridge. He is the only man ever to have crossed New York's East River on a wire.

An Open Boat

The famous American novel, *Open Boat*, by Stephen Crane, was dedicated by Crane to a native of Catalina, Captain Edward Murphy. The classic book, which later became the basis for a Hollywood movie, was based on the thirty days Crane and Murphy fought for survival in stormy Caribbean seas.

Crane met Captain Murphy while a passenger on Murphy's boat, the *Commodore*, while enroute to Cuba to work as a war correspondent in 1897. Murphy was a gunrunner between the United States and Cuba, and his many cargoes of weapons and ammunition helped the Cubans gain their independence from Spain.

On New Years Day, 1897 the *Commodore* set out for Cuba, with a cargo of guns, and an American war correspondent Stephen Crane on board. Crane was scheduled to join up with and report on the Cuban guerilla movement.

However, the ship struck a sandbar while leaving Jacksonville. Hours later, it was leaking badly and there was trouble with the engines. Captain Murphy organized his crews in an effort to save the vessel, but this failed and he ordered all on board to abandon ship.

Several of the lifeboats capsized in heavy seas, and all on board them drowned. Captain Murphy, Stephen Crane, Steward Montgomery, and Bill Higgins ended up in a dinghy.

For thirty hours, Captain Murphy, although injured, struggled to stay awake, and used his seafaring skills to keep the little craft afloat and on course for Florida. When the craft neared Daytona, it was overturned by a wave and Murphy rescued Crane when he was seized with cramps.

When Crane reported on the incident to his New York newspaper, he wrote, 'I would prefer to tell the story all at once, because from it would shine the splendid manhood of Captain Edward Murphy and William Higgins.'

Crane went on to write a book about the incident which he called *The Open Boat*. He also wrote another American classic, *The Red Badge of Courage*. Murphy, for his part described Crane as the spunkiest fellow he ever met.

Captain Edward Murphy came down with malaria and died at New York on September 3, 1898. His body was brought back to St. John's and on September 30 he was buried at Belvedere cemetery.

Hollywood Star Married a Bell Islander

A Hollywood movie star who has appeared in many movies, television features and Broadway shows, and one who once was awarded an Emmy, is the son of a Newfoundlander, and has several other interesting connections with this province.

The star served as a private in the United States Army Corps of Engineers from May 1943 to March 1946, part of which time he was stationed at Fort Pepperell in St. John's. Even at that time he showed a keen interest in acting and was an active member of a St. John's amateur theatre group. When he returned to the United States he took with him his fiance, a girl from Bell Island named Ruby Elaine Johnston. They were married at New York City on September 22, 1945 in a church called Little Church Around the Corner.

After the war he and his Newfoundland-born wife entered Denison University and the actor majored in drama, graduating with a B. A. degree with honours. While at the university, he became an expert on Mark Twain. Not only an expert on his works, he made a career out of travelling all over North America impersonating Twain and lecturing on his works. He delivered 307 performances in which he impersonated the famous American humourist.

His radio and television career began in 1952. He played the part in a television series called *The Brighter Day* on CBS. He also appeared as Mark Twain on the Ed Sullivan Show, as well as making a series of appearances on the Tonight Show.

Critics described his performances of Twain as 'miraculous', 'brilliant recreations', 'rare entertainment', and 'a perfect evening'. *Life* magazine on October 9, 1959 reported that his performance was the greatest theatrical surprise of the year. It usually took him two hours just to make himself up as Twain.

In 1959 this man performed at the White House for President Eisenhower's birthday, and during the 1960s, he played the part of Abraham Lincoln in a television movie.

Other movies in which he has played included: *Does a Tiger Wear a neck Tie?*, *The Group*, *The People Next Door*, *Wild in the Streets*, *After the Fall*, *The Man of LaManche*, and the movie which earned him his Emmy Award . . . *The Senator*. The most famous of all his performances was his part in the movie shown all over North America on Sunday night, February 8th, 1986. . . *Under Seige*. In that movie, he played the president of the United States.

By now you have probably guessed his name . . . Hal Holbrook; or, more correctly, Harold Rowe Holbrook, who was born at Cleveland, February 17, 1925. He was the son of Harold Rowe Holbrook of Connecticut and Aileen Davenport of Newfoundland and one of four children born to the couple. His mother was interested in the theatre herself, and appeared on Broadway in *Scandals* and at the Ziegfield Follies. His mother deserted the family when he was two years old and Hal was brought up by his grandparents in Massachusetts and Cleveland.

Chapter III
CRIME

Cannibalism, prison escape and murder are just some of the topics included in this chapter, which features some intriguing and amazing stories from the pages of the criminal history of Newfoundland.

Almost Cannibalism
Execution at Signal Hill
Ham-String Collins
Justice for All
The End of Mummering
Mutiny and Murder
A Rumour Out of Hand
A Murder Mystery in the Straits of Belle Isle
Prisoners must pay . . .
Prison Escape

Almost Cannibalism

The tragic happening that took place on the *Fanny Wright* during the mid-19th century is perhaps one of the most horrible to take place on the Atlantic. The *Fanny Wright* got caught up in a severe storm after leaving St. John's with a cargo for Ireland. The captain and crew, other than the cook, John Gorman, were all Irishmen. Gorman was a Newfoundlander from Water Street west in St. John's.

The ship received heavy damage during the storm and, when it subsided, the men on board were unable to get below deck because the heavy seas had flooded the cabins and storerooms. Three crewmen drowned during the battle to save the ship from sinking. The survivors were left with no food and only a small supply of port wine and drinking water. The deck was covered with water, and there was not even a dry spot for anyone to sit or lie down for rest. After 96 hours of being exposed to hunger and salt water, the men began to weaken and many of them broke out in sores.

In desperation, on the nineteenth day after the storm, the Captain suggested that the only way they could survive was to resort to cannibalism. One of them had to sacrifice himself so the others might live. The men had mixed feelings over the idea, and some were horrified at the thought. Yet the captain convinced them it would be necessary; All married men were exempt from the draw to determine who the unfortunate one would be. The choice was limited to four teenage boys. Each was given a stick of different lengths, with the shortest stick determining who would be sacrificed. A young boy from Limerick, Ireland named O'Brien picked the fatal stick.

The captain placed a bandage around the boy's eyes as he trembled. He then passed a knife to Gorman and ordered him to kill the boy. When Gorman hesitated, the others threatened to kill *him* if he did not carry out the captain's orders.

Trembling himself, he cut O'Brien's wrist, but was shocked when no blood appeared. The crew forced him to try again, and this time he slit the boy's throat. O'Brien screamed and fell dead to the floor.

Just as the men got ready to cut the boy up for a feast, a ship appeared on the horizon. It was an American vessel named the *Angenora*. The men covered the boy with a tarpaulin and the Americans took the survivors back to Ireland. Their fate has yet to be revealed by historians.

Execution at Signal Hill

The political situation in Newfoundland during the year 1800 was explosive. Fanned by reports that the British had suffered a number of defeats in Europe, and the abolition of the Irish Parliament, a group of Irish military men at Fort William developed a plan to take control of the fort and the city of St. John's.

The conspirators planned to lead an uprising during Sunday Mass on April 20, then proceed to the Protestant Church to take prisoner all the officers and leading inhabitants. Roman Catholic Archbishop, J. Louis O'Donel, an Irishman himself, had little sympathy for the Irish rebels and felt their violent activities back in Ireland were a disgrace to the Catholic Church. O'Donel learned of the plot and advised the commanding officer of the fort, Brigadier General Skerrett. When Sunday arrived, the general foiled rebel plans by sending them on manoeuvres, instead of on the usual church parade.

This action only delayed rebel plans, and, on the night of April 24, about twenty of them deserted their regiments and assembled at a powder shed on the barrens. Others from the fort were prevented from joining them after an alarm had been raised at the fort. Two days later, the rebels confronted loyal troops in the woods near St. John's. Most of them escaped; however eight were captured and tried for treason. After being sentenced to death, they were taken to Gibbett Hill near Cabot Tower and executed. Following their execution, the eight men were left hanging in chains as a spectacle and a deterrent to others who might consider rebellion.

There was strong support for the rebels among the people of

St. John's, most of whom were Irish. United Irish support was sparked around the island, and Skerret had to reinforce the garrison at Placentia. The Irish supporters were controlled by a directorate of five men. O'Donel's role in foiling the uprising is disputed by some historians; however, they acknowledge the strong possibility that he did play an important part. Most agree that he played a major role in calming the civilian population and counteracting support for the rebels from the townspeople and the garrison.

Ham-String Collins

John Collins was the official governor of Fort William in St. John's during the 18th century. He was a familiar figure around town at the time and walked with a limp. How Governor Collins got his limp is quite an interesting story.

The injury to the governor's leg was afflicted during a social visit to Reverend John Jackson's residence near the Fort. Reverend Jackson was the first Anglican clergyman to serve in St. John's. He had become infuriated by the openly disorderly conduct of Captain Lloyd, the commander of Fort William.

The Reverend sent a letter to England, complaining of his behavior and Lloyd was called home to defend himself against the charges. Jackson claimed that Lloyd abused the Lord's Day and consorted with wicked women. The Reverend suggested that Lloyd had given one Madame Short absolute power over the soldiers at the fort. Madame Short used this power to have soldiers lashed and whipped at will. While Lloyd was away, Governor Collins paid a sociable visit to Jackson's home. Present that evening were Mrs. Jackson, the Reverend's wife, and Lloyd's friends: Madame Short, Madam Binger, Madam Brown, and several others.

Governor Collins, a bachelor, immediately got himself into hot water by commenting that there was not an honest woman in all of Newfoundland. Parson Jackson, upset by the governor's provocative observation on Newfoundland women, asked the Governor what he thought of Mrs. Jackson. Collins glanced toward the Parson's wife and replied, "It's as I stated; there is not an honest woman in all Newfoundland." Reverend Jackson, angered by Collins's remark, made a move toward the Governor, but was beaten to the punch by his wife and the other ladies present. The women knocked Governor Collins to the floor, disfigured his face with their long fingernails, and the good parson's wife grabbed a large case knife and cut the ham-strings in the governor's leg. Collins limped for the rest of his life, a limp that was a constant reminder of his confrontation with Lloyd's ladies of St. John's.

Justice for All

The wife of the first Anglican clergyman to serve in St. John's, Reverend Jackson, was a hardhearted and treacherous woman. The Jackson's maid, a girl named Christine, once insulted Mrs. Jackson, and the consequences were tragic for all concerned. Mrs Jackson sent her daughter directly to Lieutenant Moodey at Fort William, and complained of the insult.

Moodey responded to the complaint by having the unfortunate girl tied to a gun and whipped repeatedly. Following the whipping, she was brought to a *wooden horse*, where the soldiers lifted her hands and, using a funnel, poured cold water down her sleeve. The soldiers then patted her back so the cold water would seep through. When this punishment was finished, she was thrown out into the cold, snow-covered forest and the local population was forbidden to shelter her. Eventually, she was taken in by Elizabeth Bunker, who gave her food and clothing.

Word that Bunker was harbouring the maid reached Fort William and Mr. and Mrs. Edward May were sent to warn Bunker that if she did not put the girl out immediately, Officer Colin Campbell would tear down the bunker house. Mrs. Bunker defied the order saying, "So what? The house is only rented anyway!"

The soldiers took no action, but a few days later, the girl died from the sickness she developed while wet and cold in the forest. Her back was black and blue from the beating and whipping the soldiers had administered.

Before dying the maid said, "God forgive those that caused me to be whipped, as I desire God to forgive me."

Captain Lloyd Collins, already humiliated and angered by Parson Jackson's complaints about him to London, returned from

England, and, when he learned of this cruelty, made some complaints of his own regarding the Jackson's.

Lieutenant Moodey and Reverend Jackson were called back to London to answer charges. They became shipwrecked off the Isle of Wight. All were saved, but the Jackson family lived in want for the rest of their lives.

The End of Mummering

Mummering is an old Newfoundland Christmas tradition that has all but disappeared from our culture. Many romantics today look upon the tradition as a quaint sort of practice which should be revived. But when mummering was a widespread practice, it was looked upon as a nuisance and a threat to public safety.

A series of incidents in St. John's and throughout Conception Bay during 1860 and 1861 finally led to the banning of mummering by Justice Carter.

During this period, there was a lot of political unrest, with riots breaking out in St. John's and elsewhere. In Bay Roberts, Isaac Mercer was attacked and murdered by a group of mummers. Inflamed by religious rivalry, that tragic event was followed by riots throughout Conception Bay.

Public pressure began to mount, led by Anglican Bishop Feild, who wrote letters to local newspapers demanding the outlawing of mummering. He referred to Mercer's murder and Christmas disturbances in St. John's as evidence of the generally disorderly condition of the colony.

An editorial appearing in the newspaper called *The Newfoundlander* argued in favour of mummering, pointing out that, 'The death of the unfortunate man was but an accidental result of the sport of Christmas mummering, and not of any deadly intent'.

Legislation banning mummering was passed on June 25, 1861 and one letter appearing in a St. John's paper noted: 'Every well-disposed citizen must be gratified at the proclamation issued by the police magistrates to suppress mummering with its disgusting attendants: rioting, drunkenness and profanity.' People were concerned that those with grudges would use the practice to

49

conceal their attacks on enemies.

A Harbour Grace doctor lead a group of mummers on an escapade in which they captured the local constable and locked him in his own handcuffs and then dropped him off at the Magistrate's house.

The practice of mummering, although outlawed, continued until the 1920's. As a matter of fact, it is still against the law, as the law has never been repealed.

Mutiny and Murder

A bungled mutiny, murder, and robbery near St. Pierre led to the arrest and hanging of the small band of men who perpetrated the crimes. The story begins in October, 1928 when the *Fulwood* set sail from Canada heading for England to purchase provisions. As was the custom in those days, the ship carried a full load of Spanish gold and other coins to make the necessary purchases. When the ship left port the gold and coins had been locked in several large chests and stored below deck.

Crew members did not become aware of the treasure on board until they had been at sea for several days. Then, they banded together and mutinied; stabbing the captain and officers and taking control of the ship. In their haste to steal the gold, the gang overlooked consideration of an important consequence of the mutiny: they had no one among them who could navigate a ship.

Between St. Pierre and Miquelon there is a stretch of sand sometimes slightly covered by water and known as 'the dunes'. Many vessels had shipwrecked at this point. With no one to navigate the *Fulwood* sailed straight into the dunes and became wrecked. The ship was sinking faster than the men could get the gold off. In desperation, they tied together some lifeboat oars to make a raft to carry the last of the gold chests. The raft broke open and the chests sank beneath the sea.

French authorities on St. Pierre investigated the sinking and discovered the murder, mutiny, and robbery that had led to it. The men were rounded up by the French police and sent to military authorities in Newfoundland. From there, they were taken to London under guard, where they were tried and executed at a public hanging near the Old Bailey Court House.

Many attempts were made to find the gold the men had managed to take off the ship. But it was not until the early twentieth century that the Uncle of Emilien Parrot at St. Pierre, while on a trouting trip, noticed a birch wall protruding from a sandy embankment. He dug at the site and found a quantity of gold. According to Emilien, her uncle told no one at the time. He took the gold to the Canadian mainland and changed it to French money and returned. He built himself an expensive home on the Island and furnished it lavishly. Emilien has two of her uncle's paintings in her own home — paintings purchased with the money obtained from the sale of the *Fulwood*'s gold.

A Rumour Out of Hand

What started out as rumours during the summer of 1876 in the Burgeo area spread throughout Newfoundland, ending up on the pages of newspapers across the island and causing an intensive homicide investigation to be launched by the police.

The incident that sparked this sensational episode in Newfoundland criminal history was the discovery of the body of John Bassett, a sixty-two-year-old English immigrant, at Burgeo. First reports out of the area indicated that Bassett had been subjected to unusual violence. His teeth were knocked out and his jaw, arm, and legs were broken. a sou'wester was fastened tightly around his neck with a fishing line. Speculation was that he had been murdered some place else and his body carried to the place it was found.

Governor John Glover offered a 400 pound reward for any information leading to the arrest of the murderer or murderers, and police inspector Carter of the Terra Nova Constabulary, set out for Burgeo to investigate.

Carter carried out an exhaustive investigation and his findings were as sensational as the first reports of the murder. After questioning witnesses,the police inspector ordered the exhumation of the body for examination. There was not a mark of violence of any sort on the body.

The inspector searched the victim's personal belongings and

concluded that Bassett had committed suicide. The police discovered that Bassett had been depressed and experiencing domestic troubles. From letters in his home, police learned that he had planned to go home to England, but was advised by his wife and son that his house there had been sold in his absence, and that it was very unlikely that he could find work.

Meanwhile, Newfoundland authorities were upset over the rumour which had gotten out of hand; and the press, which had published the false stories, called for severe penalties to deal with the rumour-mongers.

A Murder Mystery in the Straits of Belle Isle

The S. S. *Scotsman*, on a trip from London to Montreal during October, 1899, ran aground on the Straits of Belle Isle in a thick fog and was completely lost. Of the passengers on board, nine women and two children were drowned. A Mrs. Bates, a wealthy lady from Montreal managed to get off the sinking vessel and the captain arranged for two crewmembers to escort her with her valuables to the lighthouse about three miles away.

Mrs. Bates left the cove with the two crewmen and was never seen alive again. When the captain and officers arrived at the lighthouse, they expected to find Mrs. Bates, but there was no sign of her. A search of the Island failed to turn up any clue of her whereabouts, and the two crewmen who had escorted her claimed that she had wandered off into the woods.

The incident made the front pages of Montreal and an enquiry, held at Montreal with the two crewmen testifying, failed to turn up any evidence of what had actually happened to Mrs. Bates. Her friends put up a large reward for information which would lead to the truth as to what had happened.

Nothing more was heard of the case until August 16, 1902. At that time, Captain Tom McCormack and his son John were fishing at Black Duck Cove on the Straits of Belle Isle.

They had gone ashore, and wandering along the coastline discovered the body of a woman lying by the side of a small stream. The clothing was decayed and frayed by the weather; the flesh had gone clear from the bone and only a ghastly skeleton remained. Captain McCormack took the clothing and a few other items, including a silver broach and a lock of hair, back to St. John's and buried the body on the Island.

The *Evening Telegram* invited the public to view the items in an attempt to identify the body. The body was never identified and no official investigation was carried out at the place where the body had been found, nor examination of the body itself ever made to determine if the lady had died from foul play.

Somewhere along the shore at Black Duck Cove lies the body of this woman who may be the missing Mrs. Bates; but authorities made no effort ot find out. The disappearance of Mrs. Bates remains a mystery.

Prisoners must pay . . .

During the early 19th century, the Newfoundland government allowed only sixpence a day to look after prisoners at the prison at St. John's. This amount was not enough to provide even very basic subsistence for the prisoners, so the keeper of the jail, Richard Perchard, petitioned the magistrates for an increase in the prisoners' allowance.

The petition read, 'The petition of Richard Perchard most humbly sheweth that your petitioner is keeper of His Majesty's Gaol of this place [St. John's] and that he has served in that capacity about two years. That during that period it has been his misfortune to have had charge of a great number of prisoners, many of them convicted felons, of which latter he has had occasionally had to the number of eight at one time.

'That for the support of such persons your petitioner is only allowed by the district the small stipend of sixpence per day. That such prisoners being composed chiefly of labouring men, your petitioner finds sixpence a day very insufficient for their maintenance and that the bread and water with which they are supplied often cost him more than the amount of such allowance, common humanity forbidding him to increase their necessary sufferings by the cravings of hunger, but that such demands are in a certain degree an injury to the petitioner's own numerous family.

'That your petitioner is nevertheless very grateful for his appointment to the said Office, but is persuaded that when the present rate of allowance was fixed it was deemed adequate to cover all necessary expenses, which he finds it not to be.'

In conclusion the petition stated, 'Your petitioner therefore humbly prays that your worships will be pleased to take into consideration and endeavour to procure for him such additional allowance for the maintenance of prisoners in the said gaol as your worships may think reasonable . . . and as in duty bound will ever pray . . . (signed) Richard Perchard.'

The Chief Magistrate for Newfoundland turned the petition over to Governor C. Hamilton, and on October 20, 1823 a reply was received. Governor Hamilton sympathized with the plight of Perchard, but the government could not afford to increase the allowances; yet he did offer the jailer a solution. Hamilton gave Perchard the authority to charge the prisoners for their keep while they were in prison. The Governor advised that in the future, Perchard should charge each prisoner nine pence per day for board and lodging.

Two years later the Grand Jury inspected the jail and determined it had deteriorated into a very bad state of repair and was no longer suitable for the purpose for which it had been intended.

Prison Escape

During 1848 there was a world-wide search for Dermot Brady and Edward Naughton after they had robbed the Manchester Bank and escaped form England. Using the alias names 'Bradshaw' and 'O'Kelly', the two bandits slipped away from England on board the *Britannia*, a passenger liner operating between Liverpool and New York. The Novelist Charles Dickens and his wife were passengers on the same vessel, and the two robbers spent many hours chatting with them.

When they arrived in New York however, they learned that the police were searching for them there, so they fled aboard a ship called the *Northern Light*, which was heading for Fogo. By August of that year, they were in St. John's passing themselves off as the sons of Irish noblemen.

They were well-educated, experts at cards and billiards, and they talked constantly about their friend, Charles Dickens, and their trip with him across the Atlantic.

They quickly became popular throughout the city and were invited to attend all the parties and social gatherings taking place. Then one day, Naughton went into the Dublin Book Store on Water Street, owned by Bernard Duffy. He used a large banknote to purchase a book. Duffy became suspicious, and thought the note was counterfeit. He told Naughton that he was short of change and suggested he come back in an hour. Duffy took the note to Bishop Fleming, who checked it against the list of notes stolen in the Manchester Bank robbery. The number, 38456 matched!

Police were notified and the two were arrested. They were taken to the prison on Signal Hill. While there, friends sent them food packages. One package included a cake with a set of tools concealed inside.

They used these to break out of the prison. Naughton was wounded by a guard and quickly recaptured. Brady made it to the harbour and swam across. He was never recaptured. It was believed he made it to Blackhead, changed his name, married, and settled down.

Chapter IV
HEROES

Considering the small population of Newfoundland, we can hold our own and even better other places of much denser populations when it comes to acts of courage and heroism. This chapter makes no attempt to chronicle our long list of heroes; rather, it relates some interesting stories of a few of our heroes in acts that took place on land, at sea, at home, in war; and includes the story of our youngest hero — a five-year-old boy.

A Newfoundland Paul Revere
The Greatest Hero
Korean Heroes
Twice a Hero
Newfoundland Heroism
Our Youngest Hero
Hogan, the Hero
Captain William Fitzgerald

A Newfoundland Paul Revere

A young man named Thomas Scanlon of Water Street, St. John's performed a deed during the American Civil War which prevented the United States from declaring war on England. During that war England had recognized the government of the Southern States, causing public demands across the North for President Lincoln to declare war on Great Britain.

On Saturday night, June 12, 1866 the Galway liner *Prince Albert* sailed into St. John's Harbour carrying a crucial message to be delivered as quickly as possible to President Lincoln. The message was that England had changed its American policy and had decided to withdraw its recognition of the Southern government and to remain neutral instead.

The message, if delivered, would certainly stem the growing anti-British sentiment in the States, and prevent the Northern government from declaring war on the English. The situation seemed bleak when it was learned that the telegraph line at St. John's was out of order. The lines were down all the way from St. John's to LaManche. The fate of two great nations and millions of people depended on the message getting through.

Realizing the importance of the message, Thomas Scanlon, an employee of the Telegraph Office volunteered to take it by horseback to LaManche, from where it could be relayed to Washington. Scanlon started his journey on horseback and, when it became impossible to go any further by horse, he continued on foot. He walked over boglands, hills, and through streams until he reached a small bay where a ferry was in operation. But here again he ran into a delay. The ferry was on the other side of the Bay and Scanlon had to borrow a gun from a fisherman and fire it several times to attract the Captain's attention.

When Scanlon finally arrived at his destination he had to make repairs to the telegraph there which was out of order. He managed to get it working and sent out a message for relay to President Lincoln. Confirmation that the message had been received returned quickly. Scanlon's determination had succeeded in keeping Lincoln from declaring war on England.

The Greatest Hero

The greatest of all Newfoundland heroes has to be Captain William Jackman. He not only risked his life to save another's, but faced death 27 times in one afternoon to rescue all the crew and passengers from the *Sea Clipper* off the coast of Labrador.

These spectacular acts of heroism took place on October 9, in the middle of the October Gales of 1867. Jackman had been sitting out the storm in the home of a friend at Spotted Island. He felt a compulsion to go outside for a walk, and persuaded his host to join him. After walking a short distance, Jackman caught sight of the *Sea Clipper*, which had run onto a reef about 600 feet from the headland. Its bottom had been badly smashed on the jagged reef, and Jackman, being an experienced seaman, knew it could not last more that a few hours. Just a little earlier, the *Sea Clipper* had collided with a fishing vessel near Indian Tickle. The little fishing vessel sank immediately, but the crew were rescued and taken on board the *Sea Clipper*.

Captain Jackman ordered his companion to go back for help. He then removed his heavy clothing and boots and plunged into the foaming sea. He made it to the side of the vessel, and after getting his breath, offered to carry one passenger to shore. Jackman repeated this heroic act eleven times before his friend arrived back with a length of heavy rope. Captain Jackman tied one end around himself and the other around a large rock. He then continued his one-man rescue effort, showing determination, courage, and great endurance.

Fifteen more times he swam to the *Sea Clipper*, each time carrying one of the stranded people back to shore. After risking his life 26 times and saving 26 people, he was told there was still a woman on board. The vessel's captain, however, warned Jackman not to risk his life again, as she was near death and could never survive being dragged back through the rolling sea. Ignoring these warnings, Jackman plunged back into the sea and swam to the *Clipper*. This time, he had to go on board and take the woman in his arms. Although he got her to shore, she lived only long enough to thank him.

Upon hearing of the great feat of heroism, Jackman's father commented, "If he had not brought that woman to shore, I'd never have forgiven him."

Jackman himself was very modest about all the attention that was focused on him when the country learned of his deeds. After being presented with the Royal Humane Society's medal, he passed it to his wife, asking her to put it in a safe place. He never spoke of the medal again.

Korean Heroes

During April 1953, there was a three-day civic reception and a giant automobile parade to honour the arrival home to Newfoundland of two local heroes of the Korean War.

Twenty-year-old Cecil Pelley of Peter's Arm, and twenty-three-year-old Donald Lemoine of Grand Falls had earned the distinction of becoming the first Canadian soldiers from Newfoundland to win the military medal for gallantry.

Pelley earned his medal while serving with the First Battalion at Kowang San between August 8 and November 2, 1952. The area was under heavy fire from North Korean forces and keeping the communications lines open was of paramount importance to the Canadian Forces. He was assigned the responsibility of maintaining the lines. Pelley worked under heavy fire and frequent enemy bombardment and in all kinds of weather to keep the lines operating. On October 12, the enemy fire was heavier than usual, yet Pelley, showing utter disregard for his own safety, maintained his post and worked for 48 hours in very dangerous conditions. He repaired damaged lines and installed new lines. Between October 21 and October 24, the Battle of Kowang San was at its height, and again Pelley was in the thick of it keeping communications lines open. His effort maintained links with all companies in the battalion during a very critical period.

Lemoine earned his medal on April 30, 1952 when he was one of 14 volunteers assigned to capture Hill 113. The group made it under heavy fire to the foot of the hill, where Lemoine established a firm base with three other soldiers. From there he made a remarkable advance up the hill, crawling over trenches.

When the group came under heavy fire, they were forced to return. Lemoine held his ground and covered for his friends so they could make it back safely. His citation referred to this, noting 'His coolness under fire was an inspiration to his men. One soldier got shot in the stomach, and Lemoine picked him up and carried him 300 yard under enemy fire. He covered the others using grenades until they were all safely evacuated and then retreated himself.'

The awards won by the Newfoundlanders were instituted by King George V in 1916 for non-commissioned officers. When the heroes arrived in St. John's, they were given royal treatment. The railway depot was decorated. There was a parade throughout the city; a banquet at the Legion Hall; and a meeting with Premier J. R. Smallwood and Mayor Harry Mews of St. John's. An outdoor reception was held on the steps of the Colonial Building, with the 49th coastal artillery band, which had been brought in from Eastern Command Headquarters in Nova Scotia. On the third day of festivities, the medals were presented to the heroes by Lieutenant Governor Sir Leonard Outerbridge of Newfoundland.

Sgt. P. Squires, Sgt. W. Bennett, Sgt. D. LeMoine, Lt. W. Stewart, Sgt. R. Heale.

Twice a Hero

A feat of skill and bravery, which deserves to be on the long list of outstanding stories of Newfoundland heroes, took place in the waters of a gulch near Trepassey during September, 1887.

The hero of the event, Tom Neil, was alerted by his close friend John Kennedy that the cargo ship *Maglona* had gone aground nearby. When the two arrived on the jagged and steep cliffs of the gulch the weather was thick, nearly raining and the sea was wild.

The crew had risked their lives getting from the sinking vessel onto a rock in the gulch, but during the attempt, Captain Richards was thrown into the sea and swept upon a partially sunken rock. The others managed to pull him to safety. Although the entire crew had made it off the vessel, they were really out of the frying pan and into the fire. The rock on which they had climbed was 100 feet high and cut off from the main shore cliff by the gulch and swelling sea.

Neil, watching the desperate men, decided their only chance would be if a line could be gotten to them. Neil and Kennedy got a line, tied it around Neil, and without any thought for his own safety, he jumped into the water and swam towards the stranded men. Neil was tossed head over heels many times but determination kept him going until he got to the men. When the men pulled him from the water he was badly bruised and bleeding. They took the line from his waist and pulled in the heavier rope from Kennedy on shore. Then one by one they were hauled through the water until reaching the safety of land.

Following this ordeal, Neil then led the rescued men over seven miles of open, empty, cold and wet country to Cape Race.

This heroic incident had a connection with another act of courage ten years earlier when a Trepassey man was lowered by rope down a treacherous 300 foot cliff to send up the bodies of victims of the S.S. *George Washington* disaster. That man was the same Thomas Neil who risked his life to save the Captain and crew of the *Maglona*. A truly remarkable Newfoundlander.

Newfoundland Heroism

The O'Keefe brothers of Eastern Cove, Fogo District, had a very close encounter with death in 1971, and if it had not been for the courage of two Fogo men the O'Keefes would have been swallowed up by the sea.

The O'Keefes were sailing a small vessel that struck a large ice pan which damaged its bottom. Water began seeping in and the small craft began to sink slowly into the cold Atlantic waters.

About a quarter of a mile away, Nat Sheppard and his son Mark were racing back to shore to escape an oncoming storm that was expected to hit the area. When they came near the O'Keefes they were attracted by their shouts for help. The Sheppards manoeuvred their boat as close as possible to the sinking O'Keefe boat. By then the seas were getting rough and they decided not to risk transferring the men from the sinking craft.

Instead, Nat Sheppard tossed a boathook to the O'Keefes and attempted to tow them to shore. The storm began to worsen and it was apparent to all concerned that they would never make shore in time. There was no other alternative now but to attempt to remove the O'Keefes from their boat.

Nat and Mark Sheppard worked skillfully to get the first O'Keefe brother to safety but while pulling Tom O'Keefe across, the line broke, causing him to fall into the sea. At first it seemed Tom was lost. He disappeared under the water and the others felt the rolling sea would carry him away. However, he surfaced near enough to the Sheppard boat for young Mark to reach over the side and grab him by the shoulders. For a while it seemed that the effort to drag Tom on board would cause the boat to capsize, however the rescue was successful and all hands made it to shore before the full intensity of the storm hit.

In recognition of their heroism, Nat and Mark Sheppard were awarded the Carnegie Hero Commission Award for bravery on June 28, 1972. The award consisted of five hundred dollars and a medal to each person. The Sheppards are the only Newfoundlanders ever to have won that award.

Our Youngest Hero

The youngest person ever to receive the Royal Humane Society's Medal for Bravery was five-year-old Fred Kirby of Newfoundland. Young Kirby was living at Burin in 1904, the year his actions won him the award.

The harbour at Burin was completely frozen over, with the exception of one spot where the coastal steamer had cut a channel through several days earlier. It had partially frozen over, but was very thin.

Fred Kirby was among a large group of boys and girls of all ages playing in the harbour. An eight-year-old boy named Parsons skated unsuspectingly over the thin ice and it suddenly gave away beneath him.

Young Parsons' screams for help frightened the other children, causing them to race for shore. All except Fred Kirby; who moved towards the boy drowning in the water. Although only five years old, Fred realized that if some immediate help was not given, his friend would certainly drown.

Kirby skated to the edge of the broken ice and lay down on his stomach. He extended his reach and grabbed Parsons by the hands. He held tightly, awaiting help from shore. Fred grew increasingly tired and his arms began to ache, but he would not release his grip. Finally, the men from shore arrived and pulled both of them to safety.

Fred Kirby was widely acclaimed by the media for his coolness and bravery in the face of the possible loss of his friend's life. Young Kirby was invited to St. John's and given a hero's welcome. He was presented with the Royal Humane Society's Medal for Bravery by the Governor of Newfoundland, thus becoming the youngest holder of that medal in the British Empire.

Hogan, the Hero

When John Hogan of Carbonear was sworn in as a Newfoundland Ranger, he expected adventure and danger in his new job, but he never dreamed of the type of danger and challenge he was destined to face. This was an adventure that would see Hogan jump from an airplane, rescue an airforce NCO and survive 51 days in the wilderness on roots, berries, and wild animals.

The Hogan epic began on May 8, 1943 when he boarded a Canadian aircraft at Goose Bay to fly, by way of Gander, to St. John's. As the aircraft passed over the northern peninsula, the plane suddenly filled with smoke. Thinking it was on fire, the pilot ordered Hogan and three other passengers to parachute. They did, but later the pilot discovered that the smoke was caused by new paint that had only recently been applied to the plane's interior. It proved to be a very fatal mistake.

Meanwhile, Hogan landed safely and spent his first night in a lean-to which he made, using his parachute. The next morning, he tracked down Corporal Eric Butt of the Royal Air Force, who had parachuted with him. The other two passengers were never found.

When found, Butt had both feet frostbitten. Hogan carried him to a trapper's cabin where he made bandages from underwear and mixed up a homemade ointment which he used to treat Butt's feet. He refused to hike to safety himself and stayed on to help Butt stay alive. To do this he hunted wild game, gathered green leaves and roots, and kept a fire going.

The search that was being carried out for the four parachuters was called off on June 22 and they were given up for dead; but three days later, on June 25, Butt and Hogan were rescued by a surveying party and taken to Port Saunders at Hawke's Bay. They had survived fifty-one days in the rugged wilderness of Newfoundland's north.

Hogan was returned to St. John's, where he was treated for six weeks at St. Clare's hospital for exposure and exhaustion.

A year later, Governor Humphrey Walwyn awarded Hogan the King's Police and Fire Services Medal. When the force was disbanded in 1950, Hogan transferred to the RCMP. He served with the St. John's detachment as staff-sergeant, and, after retirement from the force, headed up the St. John's Harbour Patrol. He passed away during the early 1980s.

On October 18, 1983 the Newfoundland Government honoured his memory by having a mountain named after him. Mount Hogan is on the Northern Peninsula where Hogan's great adventure took place.

Captain William Fitzgerald

Captain William Fitzgerald of Harbour Grace gained international recognition during the latter part of the 19th century and was awarded special recognition by the Kaiser of Germany. Captain Fitzgerald was the son of Captain William Fitzgerald, senior, a well-known and respected sea captain during the late 19th century.

The younger Fitzgerald became a master mariner and worked for John Munn and Company, the same company that had employed his father. It was during his service with the Munns, as captain of the schooner *Rose of Torrage* that Captain Fitzgerald gained international renown. The *Rose of Torrage* was a 114 ton vessel built for Munn's in 1875 by Cox shipbuilders at Bideford.

On one voyage, when the vessel got caught in a terrible storm, Captain Fitzgerald pulled in, dropped anchor and rode out the storm. When the intensity of the storm decreased, Fitzgerald could see a ship in distress in the distance. The sea had burst open her hatches and she was slowly sinking. He manoeuvred his tiny craft alongside the German vessel, which bore the name *Casendra*. The storm had broken up all the lifeboats on the steamship and the only hope for survival for those on board was to get to the *Rose of Torrage*.

The winds were still high and the seas heavy as Fitzgerald and his crew of seven attempted to get lifeboats to the *Casendra*. It took six hours to complete the rescue of the German seamen. The Newfoundland vessel was small and had accommodations for only eight people. conditions on the vessel were overcrowded and uncomfortable, however the Germans were well-treated by the

67

Newfoundlanders and dropped off safely at Gibralter. From there, Fitzgerald continued his journey to southeast Spain with a load of fish.

The daring sea rescue received world-wide attention, and some time after his arrival back at Harbour Grace, Captain Fitzgerald received an invitation to Government House in St. John's. There the governor presented him with a special gift from Kaiser Wilhelm of Germany. The gift was a gold watch with his picture on the inside cover and the account of the rescue engraved upon it.

Some years later, Fitzgerald rescued the crew from the sinking S.S. *Wolverton*; but there was no one there to rescue *him* when the ship he skippered, the *Grace*, sank in Atlantic waters.

Chapter V

TALES OF THE SUPERNATURAL

I have selected four astonishing tales of the supernatural from Newfoundland's past to include in this chapter. These tales tell of the sudden departure of the entire community at Chance Cove; a clergyman's account of a man returning from the dead; St. Peter's telling a Bonavista Bay man the exact date he would die and a dream that saved lives.

Back from the Dead
Chance Cove Ghosts
A Prophetic Dream
A Crazy Dream that Saved Lives

Back From The Dead

Reverend F. E. J. Lloyd was a missionary in northern Newfoundland and Labrador during the latter part of the 19th century. His mission included fifty-two settlements along 200 miles of coastline, including forty miles of Labrador coast. While reviewing some of the notes he recorded in his diary, concerning events that took place during his stay in Newfoundland, I came across an interesting tale of the supernatural.

Lloyd wrote in his diary that 'On the second of December, 1883 there died in a settlement of my mission, Savage Cove, an old man of ninety years, George Gaulton by name. He was confined to bed for several months before his death, during which time I visited him as frequently as possible. I repeatedly begged him to unburden his mind to me if his conscience were with any weighty matters. But he as often assured me that all was well.'

Reverend Lloyd continued, 'On December fourth, we committed his body to the grave. On the fifteenth, George Gaulton appeared in the flesh to a former acquaintance named James Shenicks at Port aux Choix, fifty miles from where he died. Shenicks told several people of Gaulton's death a considerable time before the actual news of it arrived.'

Missionary Lloyd discussed the apparition with Shenick and recorded his account of the incident in his diary. Lloyd stated that Shenick said: 'I was in the woods cutting timber for a day and a half. during the whole of that time, I was sure I heard footsteps near me in the snow, although I could see nothing. On the evening of the second day, I returned home early. Something forced me to go to the hay pook [a small stack of hay]. While there I stood face to face with old George Galton. I was not frightened. We stood in the rain and talked for some time. In the course of the conversation, the old man gave me a message for his eldest son and begged me to deliver it before the end of March. He then disappeared and I was terribly afraid.'

Shenick set out for Savage Cove to meet with the young Gaulton and told him of his dead father's appearance and the message he asked to have delivered. Young Gaulton told Reverend

71

Lloyd that when his father died he made several unsuccessful attempts to say something and then passed away.

The final paragraph of Reverend Lloyd's diary says: 'The above is authentic. I will make no further comment upon the extraordinary occurrence but will leave it thus to the reader, who may ponder it at his leisure.'

The message brought back from the grave by George Gaulton was never revealed.

Chance Cove Ghosts

The name Chance Cove, on the Southern Shore, pops up frequently in Newfoundland history as a place where many ships were wrecked and hundreds of lives lost. Perhaps the most famous Chance Cove shipwreck was that of the *Anglo Saxon* in 1869. However, a big mystery surrounds Chance Cove and in fact even more than a hundred years after its occurrence it continues to remain a mystery.

The story, which has grown into legend, started just three or four years after the wreck of the *Anglo Saxon*. There had been rumours of strange happenings at the Cove and stories spread along the shore of ghosts and apparitions at Chance Cove.

Then the happening occurred that has remained unexplained all these years. All the families living in the settlement at that time packed up their belongings and moved out. They left their homes, barns, shed, and farms and took with them only what was moveable. There was no explanation for the sudden exodus. Chance Cove became a ghost town.

While history shows no valid reasons for the desertion of Chance Cove, people along the Southern Shore were convinced it had something to do with the supernatural. Those who knew people living there told of terrifying screaming at night, the apparition of ghosts, the cries for help. They said it was a haunted town.

They say the event that sent the inhabitants packing took place on the anniversary of the *Anglo Saxon* disaster. Late that night, the people were awakened by uncanny noises and loud and heartrending screams. They seemed so real that the fishermen got out of bed and rushed to the beach only to find nothing. Upon returning to their homes, the haunting was repeated. The next day everyone in the community left and never returned.

In 1897 a St. John's journalist, John White, paid a visit to the community. He noted that on the beach north, south, east, and west of the cove, lay portions of wrecked steamers, many of which must have gone down with some of their living freight. When a sudden wind and rainstorm erupted, White and a friend were forced to spend a night in the ghost town. They found the door to the school open and decided to spend the night there. White recalled, 'It never rained before nor since half as hard as it did that night. We never slept a wink.' White reported that he intended to visit again some day, but whether it rains hard or soft he said he would never spend another night there. He did not explain why.

Twenty-five years later, some fishermen from northern Newfoundland operating in waters along the southern shore took advantage of the vacant homes and used them as a base of operation for their fishing efforts. They too quickly left, but whatever frightened them off did not stop them from trying to fight back. The fishermen put a torch to the community before departing and destroyed every standing building.

A Prophetic Dream

Over the past years I have researched some really amazing stories from Newfoundland's past, but the story I am about to tell is in a category all its own. It is the story of Jim Powell of Bonavista Bay; a story that took place during 1890. Jim Powell has the unique distinction in Newfoundland history of knowing long beforehand, the exact date and year of his death.

Jim Powell's death was revealed to him in a dream he had. In this dream Powell felt out of place; he had a gnawing feeling that he did not belong there. St. Peter beckoned to him to follow along what seemed like the huge wall of the heavenly palace. Along the wall there was a special niche for everyone. St. Peter stopped at one of these and, turning to Powell said, "This is your crown, and three years from this date I am coming for you."

When Powell woke up, he was shaken by the prediction of

his death. He told the story to relatives and friends, and although they took the dream lightly, Powell did not. His life changed almost immediately. He became religious, and his general conduct and attitudes towards friends and relatives became more Christian. During the months that followed, Jim put up with many good-natured jokes about his time running out and the impending visit of St. Peter.

On the third anniversary of the dream, people in Bonavista were paying close attention to Powell. He was due back from a trip to St. John's. Early that morning, he was on a ship that left Baine Johnston's Wharf in the city, heading north for Bonanvista. A larger schooner that left the same time made it safely to Bonavista and reported to the amazement of all that Powell was dead. It was the exact date given by St. Peter in Powell's dream, three years earlier.

The schooner's captain reported that Powell's boat had been split in two, and that all on board, except the man at the wheel, drowned.

A Crazy Dream that Saved Lives

One of the most remarkable escapes from death in Newfoundland history took place on a capsized vessel which was returning to Codroy Valley from Labrador. The vessel carried Captain John Gollop and five crewmembers: Henry, Joshua, and Benjamin Gollop, all brothers of the captain; and Wilson Fiander and fifteen-year-old Willie Owens, the cook.

A fierce storm struck as the vessel approached Bay of Islands. A huge wave hit the ship causing it to keel over on her side. The ship did not sink, because a shipment of empty barrels kept it afloat. Henry Gollop drowned, but the others struggled to safety and tied themselves to the ship to avoid being washed away.

The storm continued with winds and waves pounding the ship and the survivors lapsing in and out of consciousness. The men, suffering cold, hunger, and exposure, expected death at any moment. Then, a strange thing happened!

Captain John awakening from his sleep, announced to the others that he had dreamt that he had made a boat from the canvas sails and then used the contraption to get to shore. At first the others were not impressed by the idea, but finally they agreed to try it out of desperation.

The men had only one knife, which they took turns using, to cut the canvas. They used the bulwark for the framing and lashed it together with rope. Then they stretched the canvas around the frame. the whole effort was a difficult and slow process because the ship was tossing in the water.

Captain Gollop was not deterred when they put the canvas boat in the water and it sank. They pulled it back on board and replaced the frame with lighter wood. This time, the thirteen by four foot canoe-shaped craft floated. They waited a few days until the winds calmed and then set out in the twenty mile journey to land, using wood from the ship as oars.

Despite some minor difficulties, they made it to a deserted fishing village at Chimney Cove and had a meal of turnips and salt cod heads which had been left there by fishermen. After resting, they got into their canvas boat and set out for the Bay of Islands. Their good fortune increased when they met up with a schooner which took them on board and brought them to Corner Brook.

The men owed their lives to the seemingly crazy dream of Captain Gollop.

Chapter VI

STORIES OF
COLOURFUL OLD ST. JOHN'S

A City of Towns

St. John's was once comprised of several smaller towns which together made up the City of St. John's. Some of the names of these towns are still familiar throughout the City, but others have disappeared and very few people today can even tell where each of them was located.

These colourful names included Dog Town, Rabbit Town, Tubrid's Town, Tarahan's Town, Georgetown, Monkstown, and Cookstown.

The best known of the many towns was probably Hoylestown which was named after Sir Hugh Hoyles, the first native son to become premier of Newfoundland under Responsible Government. Hoyles later became Chief Justice of Newfoundland. Hoylestown was at first known as Magotty Cove and was located in the east end of the city around where St. Joseph's Church is now located.

St. John's around 1900.
Courtesy — Frank 'Spotty' Baird

Cookstown was located near where the Metro Bus terminal is now operating near Parade Street and Cookstown Road. Its name had its origin in a grant of land made by the world-famous navigator Captain James Cook to a man-servant who was with him when he surveyed the Newfoundland coast in the 1760s.

Then there was Tubrid's Town, situated off Barnes Road, and just down the street from that along Bond Street over to Prescott Street was Tarahan's Town. That town was destroyed by fire during the fall of 1855.

Georgetown was named after a family of that name; and Monkstown, where Monkstown Road is located, was called after a band of Franciscan monks who taught school in St. John's during the 1860s. The monks lived in a house east of the Basilica of St. John the Baptist.

Records are not clear on where Dogtown was located but it was named so because of an infestation of dogs.

Rabbit Town, however, got its name not from rabbits but simply as the name used to refer to a rapidly growing town.

Our Stagecoach and Highwayman

During the early 19th century, a stage coach line operated between St. John's and Portugal Cove. The stage coach line was brought about by Governor Thomas Cochrane in 1822. Portugal Cove was the point where small passenger packets arrived and departed to and from ports throughout Conception Bay.

Some of the well-known coachmen of the time included Bulger, Murphy, Somers, and Bennett. The coachmen were dressed in typical English coachman style; wearing a long greatcoat with cape and a top hat. One of the coachmen, Bill Somers lost his left hand in an accident and wore a leather covering to protect the stump. This handicap however, did not prevent him from becoming a skilled horseman. With the double leather reins wrapped over his handless arm, Somers could handle four horses better than most drivers with two hands.

The first coach line was called the *Coughlan Coach-Line*. The coaches were painted red and yellow. Like the stage coaches of the wild west, passengers filled the inside; their baggage on the roof and the driver sat up front, armed with a long leather whip. As the coach made the way over the dusty dirt road, the driver would blow a loud horn to warn travellers on the road of the presence of the stage coach.

Each of Coughlan's three stage coaches had a name. They were the *Velocity*, the *Victory*, and the *Ketch*. They left the old Commercial Hotel every morning at 9 a. m. for Portugal Cove. When the passengers' packets arrived, the coaches carried the passengers to St. John's.

With a stage coach in operation we had our share of bandits and highway men. One of the most celebrated of Newfoundland highway men was John Flood, the man who held up the stage as it travelled to Portugal Cove. He was tracked down by authorities, arrested, and charged with robbery and assault. Flood was found guilty and sentenced to be hung.

On January 12, 1835 John Flood went to the gallows at the old court house in St. John's. Flood was the last person to be publicly hanged in Newfoundland.

Street car tracks being laid on Water Street. This was Water Street as it looked during Prowse's era.

Courtesy — Provincial Archives, Nfld.

Our Old Taverns

During the 19th century, the population of St. John's was small, but there was no shortage of pubs, taverns, and inns. Most business establishments in the city, including these public drinking places were identifiable by swinging signs out over their doors depicting the names of the places. The *Ship's Inn* had a sign showing a large sailing vessel; the *Red Cow* had a painting of a red cow; and the *Bunch of Grapes* had its sign illustrated with a crudely painted bunch of grapes.

While there were many inns and taverns during this period, the most colourful and romantic types included the *Bull's Inn*, the *Gamecock Inn*, the *London Tavern*, the *Calibogus House*, and the *Traveller's Joy*.

The *Calibogus House* was located on Queen's Road near the Chapel Street intersection. The actual name of the tavern was the *Fisherman*, but it became known throughout the city as the *Calibogus House* because it was the meeting place of the Calibogus Club. That was an organization founded by the pub's owner, Andy Brady, in which all club members swore not to drink any spirits except spruce beer mixed with rum; — a mixture known as 'calibogus'.

Another colourful place was the *Traveller's Joy*, located in the west end of the city and owned by a crier of the Newfoundland Supreme Court. A swinging sign over its door bore the message: 'Before the Traveller's Joy you pass, Step in and have a parting glass.' On the opposite side, facing visitors and people returning to the city was another message: 'Now that your journey's almost over, Step in, your spirits to recover.'

The most famous of 19th century taverns was the *London Tavern*. It was a large, well-equipped tavern that catered to the upper class of the city. It was at the *London* that the Benevolent Irish Society was organized and held its first meetings.

The *Gamecock Inn* was another colourful place and occupied the site where Theatre Pharmacy now stands, at the intersection

Duckworth Street during early 1890's, when many of those old taverns operated. The old courthouse is on the right of this picture.
Courtesy — Provincial Archives, Nfld.

82

of Long's Hill and Queen's Road. It was owned by an Irishman named Peter Sullivan, who conducted cockfights in the back garden of the inn. The *Gamecock* was a popular place for food and drink, as well as for the excitement of the cockfights.

Other colourful pubs included the *Golden Stag*, the *Brittania*, the *Flower Pot*, and the *Crown*.

The Glue-Pot Fire — 1846

Many historians call the great fire of 1846 the 'Glue-Pot Fire', to distinguish it from the Great Fire of 1892. The Glue-Pot Fire was so-named because it was believed that the fire had been caused by an overheated glue-pot at Hamlyn's cabinet making shop on Queen Street. Hamlyn himself, however, insisted that the fire had started in an apartment above his store.

As in the Great Fire of 1892, the Glue-Pot Fire left many people homeless. Twelve thousand people were left without accommodations, two-thirds of the city was destroyed, and property loss was estimated at three million dollars.

The fire broke out around 8:00 a.m. on Tuesday, June 9, 1846. The fire department responded, but were unable to get their waterpumps operating in time to stop the spreading flames. In the afternoon there were high winds that sent blazing brands and flankers all over the city.

Governor John Harvey went to Beck's Cove to lead the fire-fighting there. Hoping to create a fire-break, he ordered that the houses of Stabb, on the southwest border of the cove be blown up. During the dynamiting, an artillery man was killed by the explosion. The effort proved useless and the fire continued to spread. By 7:00 p.m. it was all over, and the city lay in ruins. Vats of seal oil on the waterfront had exploded, spreading the fire to several ships in port. Three people lost their lives in the fire; one of them an old man trying to save his bed from a burning building. Troops were immediately dispatched to protect property and prevent looting.

Many of those burned-out spent the night outdoors on the Government House grounds and near Fort Townshend. As in other great calamities, people from other countries were quick to respond with help. The British Government sent 5,000 pounds and the British parliament authorized another 25,000 pounds.

Queen Victoria sent a letter to the Archbishops of Canterbury and York suggesting they request help from their congregations. The response was generous, and additional help came from Canada and the United States.

One of the great tragedies of that fire was the loss of many valuable historical documents. The population of St. John's at the time was 16,000 and there were 4,200 homes.

This recent photo of Queen Street in downtown St. John's shows the street on which the 1846 fire started.

Photo — Jack Fitzgerald

The Dead Christ

The valuable sculpture under the main altar of the Roman Catholic Basilica in St. John's known as *The Dead Christ* is one of three valuable art pieces created by the famous nineteenth century sculptor, John Hogan. In addition to these works, Hogan sculpted: the statue of Daniel O'Connell in the City Hall at Dublin, Ireland; a figure of Hibernia for Lord Cloncurry; and the *Eve After Expulsion From Paradise*.

His first statue of the Dead Christ depicts Christ lying in his tomb. It had been ordered for a chapel in Cork by a Father O'Keefe. Father O'Keefe was unable to raise the money to pay Hogan and the work of art was sold for about $2,000 and placed beneath the altar at the Roman Catholic Church in Clarendon Street, Dublin.

Hogan's work was widely praised throughout Europe and the popularity of his famous statue in Dublin inspired the city of Cork to commission Hogan to execute a duplicate of the statue with some minor changes. The statue is still on display at Cork.

Hogan's third statue of the Dead Christ was his best. Bishop Mullock contracted with the famous artist to sculpt the statue for a cost of $2,000 and it was shipped to St. John's on board the *Ariel* in 1863. It was carved from the purest Italian marble. Because the marble used in the statue was almost faultless, this third work of art was Hogan's best and most perfect.

John Hogan is regarded as Ireland's greatest sculptor. He was born at Tallow County, Waterford, in the year 1800. Hogan displayed a talent for art after giving up training to become a lawyer. A wealthy Irish Lord provided him with the money which enabled him to study art at Rome. Following his Italian training, he returned to work in Ireland. There are two other works by Hogan on display at the Basilica and both were commissioned by Bishop Mullock. They are the memorials on the side walls to Bishop Scanlan and Bishop Fleming.

If you have not already viewed the work of this great artist, it would be well worth your while to drop in at the Basilica and take a look.

Prowse

The history of Newfoundland is filled with characters of all sorts, but one of the most outstanding of them all was the colourful Judge D. W. Prowse of the Central District Court, St. John's.

Prowse was well-known throughout the Island for having written the famous *Prowse's History of Newfoundland*. A copy of the original publication would now fetch as much as $750; however, when it went on the market originally, it was poorly received. Yet, the old judge never lost an opportunity to promote his works.

A common story around town at the time was that Prowse would ask a citizen appearing in his court if he had read his book. If the reply was 'Yes', a verdict was reached immediately and the case was dismissed. If the answer was 'No', the verdict was ten dollars fine of thirty days in jail.

Prowse was responsible for the building of a hospital outside the Narrows at St. John's. The hospital was meant to treat smallpox cases but it was used only twice before it burnt down in 1911. Townspeople referred to the hospital as 'Prowse's Folly'. There was no road to the hospital and access could only be gained by boat.

Prowse once learned that the students of Bishop Field College were being sent out into the woods to gather spruce boughs to decorate their gym for a Christmas celebration. The judge, who lived on Torbay Road, got wind of the plan and offered to show the boys the best spruce trees in the area.

The boys, equipped with axes and tomahawks, reported to Prowse, who pointed out a certain area that was not to be tampered with, and a large adjoining area where they could cut to their hearts' delight. The boys eagerly attacked the trees and the judge left. After an hour of destruction, a man arrived on the scene, frothing at the mouth and demanding to know what was happening. It was then that the boys learned that the judge had given them permission to destroy his neighbour's property, a man disliked by Prowse.

Prowse's Navy

Judge Prowse is best remembered in Newfoundland as a great historian, having written two and a half volumes of the famous *Prowse's History*. He was also a noted character around the Island and was once referred to as the 'Admiral of the Newfoundland Navy'.

During the 1880s the Newfoundland assembly passed the famous Bait Acts, which were meant to stop local fishermen from selling bait to foreigners, mainly the French and American fishing fleets. The principle behind the move was that without bait the foreign fishing fleets would have to give up fishing in Newfoundland waters.

To demonstrate their determination, the government assigned two small ships to a special patrol service to enforce the Bait Acts. Judge Prowse was put in charge and the vessels were each armed with a gun.

The French thought it was a great joke and referred to Prowse's fleet as the Ironclads and Prowse as 'Admiral'. During 1887, the French armed with guns and bayonettes boarded Newfoundland fishing boats at Port au Port, ordering the fishermen to leave the fishing grounds. The local men refused and the French called in a man-o-war, which forced them to remove their codtraps. Incidents like this were happening all over Newfoundland; and Prowse's two small boats could not be everywhere.

On one occasion, a fishing vessel was pursued through fog and heavy seas almost to St. Pierre. The captain of the vessel was puzzled by the chase and felt sure he was about to be overtaken by pirates. He surrendered after the little craft fired at him but was delighted when it turned out to be one of Prowse's naval vessels.

Prowse's men boarded the vessel and questioned the captain about his cargo, then allowed him to carry on. Although many considered Prowse's Navy to be a joke, it did have a deterrent effect and hastened the settlement of the French Shore question in 1904.

St. John's went through various stages in the development of public transportation. Between the era of the stage coach and the metrobus we had the street car. This photo shows a street car that ran off the tracks and crashed into Gosse's Tavern during the 1930's.

Courtesy — Provincial Archives, Nfld.

Paddy Baird and the King

King George V of England and Paddy Baird of New Gower Street once had an amusing encounter on Newfoundland's west coast during a salmon trip made by our royal visitor.

As a prince, King George was once assigned to the *H. M. S. Canada* to undergo rigorous training. The vessel visited this province and spent a week in the harbour at Sandy Point.

The prince, along with several other young naval officers took advantage of their stay to do some salmon fishing. They set out for Flat Bay Brook,which runs past the foot of Steel Mountain and was known as the best place in the area to fish for salmon.

Years later when the prince was a king and celebrating his Silver Jubilee, there was a suggestion that the brook be renamed 'King George's Brook', but no action was taken on this. While on the west coast however, a special train was sent out to accommodate the prince. One of the crewmen on the train was Paddy Baird of New Gower Street in St. John's. Just before the train arrived, Paddy and his friends were discussing the proper way to address a prince.

One suggested 'His Royal Highness'. Another said just 'Prince' would do. A third suggested that 'Sir' would be proper.

When the train arrived a bunch of young eager cadets from the *H. M. S. Canada* went aboard the train. Paddy thought this would be a good time to find out how to address the prince. Paddy asked, "Tell us, how do you address the prince?" The cadets looked at each other and laughed.

One of them asked, "What do you think he should be called?"

Paddy answered, "I don't know but one thing would be as good as another. I suppose I would call him Albert; that is his name you know."

"Yes," said the future king of England," that is my name: Albert. How is salmon fishing out this way?"

Everyone had a good laugh, even the red-faced Paddy Baird.

The Riots

During 1932 Peter Cashin made accusations of government corruption in the Newfoundland legislature which led to a public enquiry and the famous riots of 1932 in St. John's. Cashin accused Richard Squires of taking $5,000 per year from the funds of the war reparations commission; St. Barbe MHA Walter Skeans of forgery; and agriculture minister Dr. Alex Campbell of deliberately avoiding paying income taxes.

The opposition demanded and got an enquiry into the allegations. At Squires' suggestion, the enquiry was headed by Governor Middleton. While Middleton concluded that the accusations were unfounded, sufficient information came out in the course of the enquiry to discredit Squires and his government, resulting in the resignations of four cabinet ministers.

The opposition was not satisfied with Middleton's findings and called a public meeting at the Majestic Theatre. Two thousand people turned up for the meeting and began a march on the Colonial Building. Word of the march spread throughout the city and by the time the protesters arrived there were 10,000 people taking part.

The mob was orderly at first and sent a delegation into the building to meet with Prime Minister Squires. Had Squires accepted their petitions, the riot could probably have been avoided. Instead, the Prime Minister sought legal advice on the legality of the delegation. When the crowd learned of Squires' delaying tactics, they stormed the Colonial Building, smashing windows and wrecking furniture. In the legislative library, they found a piano, which they carried over to Bannerman Park and destroyed. Two unsuccessful attempts were made to burn the building, and the mob finally withdrew after wrecking the entire interior of the Colonial Building and leaving it in shambles.

At 7:30 p.m., with the crowd dispersing, friends tried to get Squires away in a waiting car. Someone in the crowd recognized him and shouted to the others. Squires jumped out of the car and ran into a house on Colonial Street, out the back door, over the fences, to Bannerman Street, where he made a getaway in a passing taxicab. He escaped and hid out at a friend's house on Waterford Bridge Road.

The riot continued into the night with the crowds breaking into the city liquor stores by chopping down a telephone pole, which they used to batter their way inside.

The governor called on the Royal Navy Warship *H.M.S. Dragon* to stand by in case of further rioting. War veterans were called to duty to help the police. The riots stopped, but in the subsequent election the Squires government was defeated at the polls with Sir Richard himself being personally defeated.

Captain Douglas Fraser

Captain Douglas Fraser, one of the early aviation pioneers of Newfoundland history showed as much courage and daring in his exploits as any of those who made the numerous trans-Atlantic attempts from Newfoundland. Fraser and Arthur Sullivan, flying their famous *Gypsy Moth*, made the first airmail flight from mainland Canada to Newfoundland on November 19, 1930. The duo flew from Toronto to Mount Pearl in the single-engine plane, which had only fixed landing wheels because they could not afford to purchase pontoons. In order to buy pontoons, Fraser later resorted to taking passengers on flights over the city for $5.00 each.

The flight took 15 days, 17 hours of flying time. Heavy fog caused delays. When they crossed the Gulf they landed at a small field at Stephenville. Their next stop was a vegetable garden at Grand Falls, and their final stop was Glendenning Farm on Brookfield Road. The ironic aspect of the flight was that Fraser was not aware the plane carried mail. He first learned of its special cargo when Sullivan announced to the crowd that had gathered at the farm to welcome them, that he carried with him mail from Canada. Fraser had been a stickler over the plane; carrying only the exact weight specified by the manufacturers.

Over the following years, Sullivan and Fraser flew all over Newfoundland and Labrador in their little craft. Fraser carried out surveys that led to the building of Gander International Airport as well as the airports at Stephenville and Argentia. He had recommended the building of Gander airport and was the first person to land there when it opened on January 11, 1938.

On May 23, 1931 Fraser, then operating his own company, known as the Old Colony Airways Limited, conducted an unusual search. Accompanied by Dr. Cluny MacPherson, he searched the Newfoundland coast for a dog. The dog belonged to Hollywood movie producer Varrick Frissell, who had died in the *Viking* disaster. Fraser had been hired by Frissell's father after receiving reports that Varrick's dog was wandering along the coast near the disaster site. Dr. Frissell thought that finding the dog might lead to the rescue of his son. Fraser searched the area and returned to St. John's to report that the search had been unsuccessful.

After Fraser's partner, Sullivan, was killed in a plane crash near St. Anthony, Fraser joined British Imperial Airways, becoming their first pilot in Newfoundland. Fraser and his mechanic assembled the two Gyspsy Moth planes sent by B.I.A. to their new branch. Fraser also set up Botwood as a major base for the trans-Atlantic flying boat operations of the early 30s.

His final act as a pilot was to take part in the search of the Musgrave Harbour area following the crash of the plane carrying Sir Fredrick Banting, the co-discoverer of insulin. He brought Banting's briefcase and personal belongings back to St. John's.

The Rebel

Kevin O'Doherty was one of many Irish patriots during the late nineteenth century. He was captured by the British in 1868 and sentenced to banishment from Ireland for seven years. At the time of his sentence, he was in love with Eva Marie Kelly of Dublin, who was then considered a great Irish poet and was referred to throughout the British Isles as the Poetess of the Nation. When he left Ireland's shore for destinations unknown, Eva was there to promise him that she would wait for his return.

O'Doherty was on a ship heading for St. John's, Halifax, and Boston, and had the choice of staying in either city. He chose St. John's. However, he decided to keep his name and past a secret, so he assumed a new name, and settled on a piece of land on Topsail Road, not far from Bowring Park. He constructed a little tilt and kept to himself. The local people did not bother him there because they thought the tilt was haunted.

O'Doherty himself was considered a hermit and had no friends. He survived by selling the products of the forest and stream and was a well-known figure around the city as he peddled these products. The local people had no idea who he was. In appearance, he was young and handsome and had a splendid physique and a pleasing personality.

One written account of the man simply known then as the 'Topsail Road Hermit', stated that, 'His manner proclaimed the gentleman, and he would never accept charity, taking money only for the goods for their exact value. Without being melancholy, he seemed to revert to a memory that was not happy, and his habitual appearance kept distant any intimacy that might have been offered.'

When his time was up, the Topsail Road Hermit dressed in fine clothing and jewellry and boarded a ship for Ireland. Eva Mary Kelly, Ireland's great poet, was there waiting for him and the two married.

It was years after his departure that some local Irish inhabitants of St. John's learned his secret.

Nelson in St. John's

Admiral Horatio Nelson, acknowledged as being one of the greatest seamen of all time had two connections with Canada. He once spent a few weeks in Quebec, and, on another occasion, several days in Newfoundland. Nelson was not too impressed with St. John's. In a letter home to England, he described it as a most disagreeable place.

Nelson was forced to seek shelter in St. John's Harbour during May, 1782. At that time, he was in command of the H.M.S. *Abbemarie*, which he had sailed from Cork, Ireland, as part of an escort to Quebec of a convoy of merchant ships.

When the convoy arrived on the Grand Banks, the fog was so thick that Nelson ordered his crew to beat the drums and ring the ship's bell continually so the convoy ships could keep as near to each other as possible. Despite these efforts, the ships scattered in all directions.

Nelson took his vessel to St. John's Harbour to seek shelter. While there, he and his crew spent many pleasant hours at a place called the Ship's Inn, which commanded an excellent view of the harbour.

The tavern sported an outdoor sign which was a painting of a full-rigged ship. The Ship's Inn was the most popular seafarers' resort in St. John's, and occupied the site near the War Memorial now occupied by the Crow's Nest.

When the weather improved, Nelson took on fresh water and supplies for his vessel, and then sailed on for Quebec. Nelson, who defeated Napoleon's navy and was mortally wounded at Trafalgar, has more monuments erected to his memory that any other British military figure. There is a monument in Trafalgar Square in London which was completed in 1844; and another in the West Indies; three at Bridgetown, Barbados; one at Antigua; one at Notre Dame Street, Montreal, which is possibly the first monument erected to his memory; and there are many other places which have honoured the Admiral's memory.

There is a plaque on the door of Admiral's House, Antigua, which states 'Nelson lived Here'; but we have no reminder in Newfoundland that the greatest British naval hero ever visited.

Black Slaves

Black slavery is usually associated with the southern United States, but you may be surprised to learn that there was black slavery practiced right here in Newfoundland. I have had some people from the Southern Shore area tell me that they have heard old-timers tell of black slaves being owned in some areas along the shore during the early 19th century. I have searched old records looking for documents to support these claims, and I have come up with some fascinating information.

Surprisingly, the slaves were the property of a very prominent Newfoundlander at the time. The man who owned the slave family, consisting of a black woman and her two children, had moved to New Brunswick from the United States after that country declared its independence. In New Brunswick, he became a printer and from there moved to St. John's, where he founded the *Royal Gazette*.

John Ryan, a noted British loyalist, treated the slave family well during the time he controlled and owned them. However, upon his death, he left a will outlining his wishes regarding the family. The will read: 'I will and bequeath my female slave Dinah, her freedom immediately after my death; and that her two children, Cornelius and Rachel, be retained in the service of my family, or bound out to some creditable person until they come to the age of 21, then to enjoy their freedom.'

In 1772, British Courts decided that once a slave put foot on British soil, he was to be set free. However, in 1791, a further law, the Wilberforce Bill, prohibiting the further importation of slaves into Britain was defeated in the Commons.

It was not until March 25, 1807 that the law on slavery became clear. At that time, Earl Grey introduced a bill abolishing slavery. It received royal assent and became law effective January 1, 1808.

Alexander Graham Bell

Alexander Graham Bell, inventor of the telephone and the phonograph record, was on board the *S.S. Hanovian* when it struck the rocks at Portugal Cove on the Southern Shore and sunk. There was no loss of life, and Bell, along with his wife and three children, was taken to St. John's. While in the city they stayed at the Atlantic Hotel, which stood on the site now occupied by the Sir Humphrey Gilbert Building.

Although Bell invented the telephone and became a wealthy man from profits made of his invention, he actually did not like the telephone. He thought it was one of the rudest inventions ever thought up by man. Bell described his feelings saying, "Nobody but a telephone caller would interrupt you while you were having dinner, sleeping, or taking a bath."

Bell developed the idea for the telephone while living at Brantford, Ontario, but found it necessary to go to the United States to make it and have it accepted. Although he first tried to get Canadian backing, he was not successful.

Hon. George Brown, one of the fathers of Confederation, promised him $25.00 per month for six months in return for half rights to the invention. However, after a month, Brown became convinced the idea could not work and stopped payments to Bell.

The first call made using the telephone was made by Bell in Boston, and the world's first long distance call took place between Brantford and Paris, Ontario, — a total of eight miles.

When the inventor first suggested the idea for a telephone in public in Boston, a newspaper there claimed he should be arrested for claiming to make it possible to talk through a wire. However, once the invention proved practical, everyone seemed to want credit for its invention. Bell successfully fought off six hundred lawsuits from people claiming he had stolen their idea.

An oddity of Bell was that he would not sign an autograph, and when signing a letter, would always write 'sincerely' and his name as close to the end of his letter as possible, to avoid anyone inserting a sentence.

Bell had a further connection with Newfoundland. His father once lived in St. John's and was employed at McMurdo's Drugstore on Water Street.

General Balbo's Visit

Mussolini's General Italo Balbo led an armada of seaplanes across the Atlantic in 1933. The feat shook the western hemisphere into realizing the dangers of mass warfare and also opened the way for worldwide commercial aviation. This famous event in world history brought Balbo, his fleet of twenty-five seaplanes, and the 115-man crew to Cartwright, Labrador, Shoal Harbour, and St. John's.

The general and his armada arrived at Shoal Harbour on the last leg of their spectacular flight which took them from Orbetello, Italy to the Century of Progress Exhibition in Chicago and back to Italy; a total distance of 12,000 miles. This, however, was not Balbo's first crossing to America as he had already made a trans-Atlantic flight from Africa to South America. What made this crossing special was the fact that it was the largest armada of planes ever to make such a crossing. The crossing, while successful, was marred by two tragedies. Two of the seaplanes were lost, resulting in the deaths of two pilots.

The planes were constructed by the General Aviation Corporation and powered by two Pratt and Whitney Wasp Motors which were capable of one hundred miles per hour, even in the face of bad weather that would have grounded other aircraft at the time.

The planes had an eleven hundred mile range without refueling. The Italian Government sent the Italian Yacht *Alicia* with mechanics and fuel for the armada. The *Alicia* was docked on the north side of St. John's Harbour while Balbo was in Newfoundland. While the armada waited for the weather at Shoal Harbour to improve so they could continue on to Italy, Balbo and his men travelled to St. John's by train, where they were made guests of Hotel Newfoundland.

The Newfoundland Government presented Balbo and his crew with special gifts to honour their visit. The general was given a silver mounted caribou and his officers fish-shaped ashtrays.

When the armada arrived at Rome, there was a frenzy like that of an ancient Roman triumph. The adventure had cost the Italian Government one million dollars, and, along with increasing Italy's world prestige, it succeeded in diverting public attention away from the country's economic troubles.

Mussolini honoured Balbo by making him an air marshall and presenting him with a gold medal. The others were given silver medals and promoted on rank.

From Rome the new Air Marshall Balbo wrote a letter to the St. John's *Daily News* stating, 'I am glad to be able to entrust to the *Daily News* a greeting of friendship and fellowship for the people of Newfoundland. The feeling for hospitality of Newfoundlanders is supreme.'

Unclaimed Fortunes

The passage of time and the loss of old documents had caused a number of Newfoundlanders to lose their right to inheritances, in some cases worth millions of dollars. The most spectacular and fascinating of the many stories of lost inheritance includes the hundred million dollar Churchill Estate and the half million dollar Tucker Estate.

If the heirs to the Churchill fortune could ever prove their claim, the ownership of most of the property on Water Street would be placed in question. In the case of the Tucker Estate, some of those claiming to be heirs went so far as to try to pressure the Pope to intervene.

The Churchill Estate had its origins with the arrival in Newfoundland in the 18th century of Sam Churchill, who, over twenty years, accumulated land along the St. John's Waterfront, throughout Conception Bay, and Ochre Pit Cove. His fortune grew even larger with accumulations of property in England.

Sam had two daughters; Elizabeth and Clermont, and one son; Nicholas. Sam disinherited Clermont for marrying the captain of one of his fishing vessels. Elizabeth also lost her claim by marrying a man from Ochre Pit Cove.

When Sam Churchill died, Nicholas inherited everything, but didn't live long enough to enjoy his new wealth. On a trip to London, he was captured by pirates, robbed, and forced to walk the plank. The Churchill fortune then passed to Nick's daughter, with the condition that upon her death the estate go to his two sisters in Newfoundland.

This unusual stipulation was no doubt the cause for that estate remaining unsettled until this day, because Lady Churchill, daughter of Nicholas, passed away, she left her own will, leaving everything to her own children.

The multi-million dollar estate remained unclaimed until 1911 when descendents of the Churchills living in New York made claim to it. By that time, possible heirs to the fortune had grown to include hundreds. In Brooklyn, an association of Churchill descendents was formed to seek legal control over the estate. In Newfoundland, about two hundred heirs met at British Hall in St. John's. Many of them mortgaged their homes in order to make a claim on the estate.

Meanwhile, the Churchill family in England, which included the family of Sir Winston Churchill, appointed a member of the family, the Duke of Marlborough, to try and finalize disbursement of the estate. The Duke sent a lawyer to New York and Newfoundland and the lawyer was impressed by many of the claims. On one of his trips across the Atlantic, the lawyer carried with him documents relating to the estate. However his journey was never completed. The passenger ship on which he travelled, the *Titanic*, sank off the coast of Newfoundland. If the *Titanic* were ever raised and these documents were found, a lot of current

97

owners of property along the St. John's waterfront could be out a lot of money.

* * *

My second story of a great inheritance is that of a half million dollars left by Lord Tucker, whose heirs had settled in Newfoundland. Although considerably smaller than the Churchill Estate, descendents of Lord Tucker have also tried to claim it for generations.

The Tucker Story had its beginning similar to the Churchill story, with Lord Tucker disinheriting his daughter, Lady Alice, because she had married an Irish footman named Pat Molloy against his will. Pat took his wife to Newfoundland, settled at Trepassey, and founded the Molloy family there. When Lord Tucker died, he left his estate to his son, who, like Sam Churchill's son, died shortly after receiving the inheritance. He left the estate to his sister, Lady Alice, whose whereabouts were unknown.

Around the turn of the century, Archbishop Howley, Roman Catholic Bishop of St. John's, learned of the fortune, and over a number of years compiled a geneology of the Molloy family in Newfoundland which proved that Mrs. Alice Molloy of Trepassey was in fact, Lady Alice Tucker. It was Howley's efforts that saved the fortune from reverting to the Crown after not being claimed for one hundred years.

Following Howley's revelation, people claiming to be heirs of the fortune surfaced all over the world. When Archbishop Howley refused to provide his geneology charts to any of them, they petitioned the Pope asking him to order the release of the documents.

The Pope replied that he left such matters solely for the bishops to decide. A series of claims appeared in English courts, but no one established legal title to the Estate. During the 1960s, the King family of Cape Breton, Nova Scotia, made a claim on the estate and the Trepassey family of John Halleran also claimed to be descendents of Lady Alice Tucker.

Neither estate was ever settled.

Rabbits Rendell

Stephen Rendell is remembered in Newfoundland history, not because of any great political accomplishments, nor any great feats of strength or heroism. Rendell earned his place in history because he was the man who introduced rabbits to Newfoundland. Prior to 1870, there were no rabbits in this province. There were some arctic hares, which came to the island on their own, by crossing from Labrador, over the ice on the Straits of Belle Isle, but no rabbits.

Rendell was aware that rabbits were plentiful in Nova Scotia, and felt that their introduction to Newfoundland would be a valuable addition to the wildlife on the island. Rendell was president of the Newfoundland Agricultural Society at the time, and was also a well-known merchant in town. W. F. Rennie, another merchant, shared Rendell's enthusiasm toward the rabbit project, but expressed concern over whether the rabbits would survive being transplanted from Nova Scotia.

As an experiment, Rendell had four rabbits crated and shipped by schooner to St. John's. When it was certain they could survive the trip, Rendell began bringing them here on a large scale. Forty crates, carrying a hundred rabbits at a time, were imported over a four-year period.

Upon being received in St. John's, Rendell would inspect them, and then ship them to magistrates in all areas of the province. Each magistrate arranged for people in the community to bring the rabbits into the woods and set them free. Laws were enforced to protect the rabbits. People were ordered not to shoot them or interfere with them. This protection lasted for ten years, and during that time they quickly multiplied all over Newfoundland. Our climate was favourable for their survival, and there was plenty of food for them. Rendell's effort added thousands of dollars annually to the natural wealth of this province.

In addition to rabbits; sparrows and pigeons were not native to Newfoundland. They were brought here by the crews of foreign vessels. Frogs came to Newfoundland in the hay of schooners from P.E.I. and Nova Scotia.

Chapter VII
THREE FAMOUS SONG WRITERS

In almost any corner of the world you will find a Newfoundlander, and whenever you find a Newfoundlander you'll hear a Newfoundland song. Over our 500 year history, hundreds of ballads and folksongs have been written, but three of the best known and most popular are Otto Kelland's *Let Me Fish Off Cape St. Mary's*; Art Scammell's *Squid Jiggin' Grounds*; and Johnny Burke's *The Kelligrew's Soiree*.

Otto Kelland
Art Scammel
Johnny Burke

Otto Kelland

Many people consider the ballad, *Let Me Fish Off Cape St. Mary's* as the most beautiful of all Newfoundland folksongs. It was written by Otto Kelland, who was born at Lamaline, worked most of his life in St. John's, but had a great admiration for the fishermen of Cape St. Mary's.

During July, 1986 Kelland signed a contract with Columbia Pictures giving them the rights to publish, record and distribute his splendid song.

Kelland was motivated to write the famous ballad by an incident which took place in Boston in 1922. At that time, Kelland was a crew member of the S.S. *Sable*, a freighter operating between St. John's, Halifax, and Boston.

Recalling the incident, Kelland noted, "One day we were docked at East Boston. A man came aboard and asked to be allowed free passage back to Newfoundland because he was broke. The captain told him it was against company rules. When the young man suggested that he could stow away, the captain said that would be against the law and if he tried, he would be arrested."

It was the man's reply to the captain that impressed Kelland and led to his writing *Let Me Fish Off Cape St. Mary's*. The man answered the captain by saying, "I am from Placentia Bay and I'd rather be fishing on one meal a day than be up here getting three square meals of grub."

Kelland recalled, "I always admired the fishermen of Cape St. Mary's. They were great sailors and great fishermen."

In 1947, twenty-five years later, Kelland was serving as Warden at Her Majesty's Penitentiary in St. John's. One afternoon while some nuns were showing movies to the prisoners and Kelland was waiting to escort the nuns out, his thoughts turned back to 1922 and that Cape St. Mary's fisherman. He began writing and the words just flowed. It was pure inspiration. Without any rewriting, revisions or hesitation the classic *Let Me Fish of Cape St. Mary's* was born. Although Kelland never studied music, he was a capable musician. That night at home he picked up his fiddle and with as much ease as it took to write the words, Kelland composed the music for his magnificent song.

The ballad was first published as a poem in the St. John's *Evening Telegram*. When Gerald S. Doyle, who collected Newfoundland folksongs and published them heard Kelland's new song, he predicted it would become one of Newfoundland's greatest ballads. The song was first broadcast on the 25th anniversary of Gerald S. Doyle Limited and was sung by Jim Rooney.

Since then it has been sung all over the world. A Newfoundland nun walking along a street in New York was surprised to hear the song being sung from inside a nearby school. She went into the building to inquire, and discovered that the choir singing the ballad was being directed by a teacher from Lamaline, Otto Kelland's home town.

Kelland, a former superintendent of Her Majesty's Penitentiary, recently had his book, *Dories and Dorymen* published. He is a prolific writer of Newfoundland stories and songs. He has written a dozen or more including: *We Will Always Have Our Sealers, The Note in the Bottle,* and *Captain Bob Bartlett.* He also wrote *The Anchor Watch,* a collection of his poems and songs; and has two books pending publication. He plays the fiddle and accordian and his ballads have been recorded on a number of long-playing records.

Otto Kelland is also a recognized expert model shipbuilder. He spends his time in retirement making ship and dory models and writing. Surprisingly, his greatest pride is not his classic *Cape St. Mary's* but the many ship models built over his lifetime.

Art Scammel

Art Scammel wrote many Newfoundland folk-songs and ballads, but his best-known effort was *The Squid Jiggin' Ground* which he wrote at the age of 15 while living at Change Island, Notre Dame Bay. Scammel studied at the old Memorial University on Parade Street and went on to earn a degree at McGill University in Montreal. Finding it difficult to get a job as a teacher during the latter depression years, he moved to Montreal, where he became head of the English department at Mount Royal High School.

He wrote: *The Coaker, The Caplin Head, The Shooting of the Bawks,* and *The Squid Jiggin' Ground;* the best-known of his many songs, having been recorded by many groups and individual artists including Hank Snow. During ceremonies welcoming Newfoundland into Confederation in 1949, Scammel's *Squid Jiggin' Ground* was played on the Carillon bells from the Peace Tower in Ottawa.

Originally, Scammel put a tune to the song that he had heard sung at house parties in his home town. Later, well-known Newfoundland entertainer and speaker Bob McLeod adapted music from an Irish jig to Scammel's words and the folksong spread rapidly. It was first published in Gerald S. Doyle's collection of Newfoundland folksongs.

The Shooting of the Bawks, was written by Scammel just after Confederation, in protest over new Canadian laws which prohibited Newfoundlanders from shooting migrating birds; which many people depended on at that time for food. The song was recorded and Newfoundland M.P.s at the time played it in the House of Commons during debate over exempting Newfoundlanders from the shooting regulations.

In addition to his song-writing, Scammel is known and respected throughout Newfoundland for his speaking ability and wit. When he was told that *The Squid Jiggin' Ground* was being sung in Israel he commented, "I know how it got there. Some of my pupils in Montreal were Jewish and they must have carried it on some of their visits to that country. Now if only we could get the Arabs and Israelis to sing it over a bottle of Newfoundland Screech, maybe we could have a little more peace in the Middle East and a little more oil flowing westward!"

On another occasion, he got a letter from a Winnipeg radio station asking permission to use 'The Squid Diggin' Ground'. He said he was tempted to write back and ask them what sort of fish they caught in their wheat pool.

Scammel returned to live in Newfoundland in 1970 after spending 28 years teaching in Montreal.

Johnny Burke

The best-known of all Newfoundland showmen and entertainers during the early 20th century was Johnny Burke, 'the Bard of Prescott Street'. To the majority of Newfoundlanders at the time, Burke seemed like a combination of Shakespeare, Mark Twain, and the Wandering Minstrel. The late supreme court justice of Newfoundland, Jimmy Higgins once described Burke saying: 'He made his audiences laugh and cry; what artist can do more?'

In one of his ballads, *The July Fire*, he described the hero rushing to the scene of the fire only to be partly burned himself. Burke amusingly described the hero's plight:

> The whiskers that I prized,
> on that very morning died.
> I was burned as clean as any grove of birch
> and my head was shaved as clean
> as a blackened boiled crubeen
> Like a man that was going to study for the church.

Burke wrote many ballads and songs. The best-known include: *The Kelligrews Soiree, The Wedding at Renews, Trinity Cake*, and *Since Murphy Broke the Pledge*. Newfoundland singer John White has produced an interesting book featuring Burke's many compositions.*

Burke was born, probably at 10 King's Road, in St. John's during 1851. He was the son of the famous sealer and master mariner, Captain John Burke. Johnny Burke was also the cousin of Archbishop Howley. His father and his brother Bill went down on the *Nautilus*, which was shipwrecked at Petty Harbour Motion on January 1, 1865. After the death of his father, Johnny, his brother Alex, and a sister Sarah, were raised by their mother.

---

* From *John White's Collection of Johnny Burke Songs*, Harry Cuff Publications.

He had a checkered working career which included being a grocer, auctioneer, agent, door-to-door salesman, pamphleteer, movie theatre owner, and producer of dancing competitions, operas, and so on. He wrote comedy, tragedy, and light opera. His ballads, skits, and come-all-ye's immortalized events and heroes of Newfoundland.

Burke had a following that eagerly awaited each new ballad. The ballads were sold on street corners and door to door at a penney each. People brought them to the outports and gave them to the local reciter, and pretty soon all of Newfoundland was listening and singing the newest Burke ballad or song.

Chesterton once said that there are two worthwhile things in life: laughter and the love of a friend. By these standards, Johnny Burke achieved much in life. Burke appealed to the ordinary people and was an expert at expressing their simple sentiments.

His works included many of the words and phrases in use here during the early twentieth century. Words like 'heel' for rum; 'joisies' for children; 'coadys' for playing-cards; and 'hardware' for spirits.

The famous bard died in 1930 and what finer tribute could be paid him than that the one uttered by Justice Higgins, 'There came none to replace him.'

Chapter VIII
NATIVES

The original natives of Newfoundland, the Beothucks and Eskimos, were considered as oddities by early settlers. Promotors took Eskimoes on American and European tours and charged public admission fees to view them. In St. John's a captured Beothuck woman was put on display at Government House. This chapter gives a brief glimpse of this exploitation of native people as well as the fascinating story of Jens Haven, a man who laboured for years to help the Eskimos of Labrador.

The Squaw at Government House

Government House in St. John's was once used to put a captured Beothuck woman on display for local society people. This event took place on September 17, 1803. The woman, about 23 years of age, had been captured by William Cull of Fogo, as she paddled a canoe up the Exploits River looking for birds' eggs. Cull brought the woman to the Governor in St. John's. Since many unsuccessful efforts to communicate with the Beothucks had been made, the presence of a live Beothuck in St. John's aroused widespread public curiosity throughout the city.

The Governor hosted a reception at Government House on Military Road to give the local community leaders and society people the chance to meet the Indian lady in person. On the night of the reception, the Governor escorted the young woman into the reception area where she walked to the centre of the floor and took a squatting position, tightly clutching a bundle containing her clothing and personal items. She was treated well by her captors, who gave her clothing, jewellery, and food, and acted courteously towards her. Yet, she resisted all efforts to take her bundle away. She was described by one local writer as being an attractive copper-coloured woman with black eyes, and hair much like that of a European. She showed a passionate fondness for children at the event and the guests were astonished by her presence. She, in turn, was fascinated by the musicians and indicated her desire to meet them. She was escorted across the hall to the band, but resisted offers to dance by several local men. When she visited city stores the next day, she was allowed to take whatever she wished without paying.

Meanwhile, the Governor decided that it would be in the best interests of developing peace with the Indians if the girl were returned to her people. The Governor ordered Cull to escort the girl safely back to her tribe and awarded him fifty pounds for his trouble.

While some people suspected that Cull had killed the girl and

111

had stolen the gifts she was carrying back to her people, Cull claimed that he brought the girl back to where he had found her; and that she was pleased to be set free. When he returned, ten days later, she was gone, and he felt that she had returned to her people.

Eskimos on Display

Early settlers to Newfoundland viewed the Indian and Eskimo inhabitants of the Colony as a sort of oddity. There are many recorded incidents of Europeans bringing some of these native people back to Europe to be put on public display. One such incident took place during the 1880s when a group of Eskimos were taken to Europe, against the will and strong protests from the Moravian missionaries on the Labrador coast.

The group of eight men, women, and children were taken on a tour of Germany and France, and although they had been well-treated by their captors, they contracted the dreadful smallpox disease and in several months they were all dead.

One of the Eskimo men wrote the Moravian missionary at Labrador, telling him of their sad fate in Europe. He stated, 'I write to you very sadly, and am very much troubled about my relatives, for my child lives no more. She has died of the bad smallpox. By our child's death, my wife and I are strongly reminded that we too must die. My child was seen by many doctors. These men can indeed do nothing, so we will above all look to Jesus, who died for us, as our physician.

'I wish I could tell my people beyond the sea how kind the Lord is. Our master buys much medicines for us, but all seems useless. My tears come often, but the words which the Lord has spoken always brings me fresh comfort.

'I am a poor man like the dust. It is very cold in Paris, but our master is very kind to us. The Lord be with you all.'' The letter was signed Abraham, husband of Ulrikia.

The same fate of smallpox and death also faced a group of natives taken from Newfoundland to Europe a hundred years ago. In 1893, fifty-seven Eskimo men, women, and children were taken to the Chicago World Fair and were returned to Newfoundland in absolutely destitute condition.

A schooner had taken them from their Labrador homes but left them off near Stephenville to get home as best they could. On their return, they brought an epidemic of typhoid with them which spread to settlements near Hopedale. At Nain, with a population of 350, ninety died in one week. Their bodies were frozen in snowbanks until the winter thaw, when the ground could be opened up for burial.

Mary March

John Peyton was angry after discovering that a party of Beothucks had raided and stolen much of his personal property at Twillingate. Peyton, a planter and merchant of that community, was a strong-willed Newfoundlander and was determined to recover his stolen property from the Beothucks.

Just seven years before the Peyton expedition, Captain John Buchan of the Royal Navy made an attempt to open communications with the Beothucks. On that occasion, he left two royal marines in the Beothuck camp as hostages, and upon his return with additional presents, found his men murdered and headless.

When Peyton set out on his journey he had a dual purpose. He hoped to recover his belongings, and to establish friendly communications with the Beothucks. Before setting out for the Beothuck encampment at Red Indian Lake, Peyton briefed his men on how they should act in the presence of the Beothucks. He told them not to fire on the Indians under any circumstances, but, in the event he could not meet them on friendly terms, he was prepared to take prisoners.

While crossing a river near Red Indian Lake, a herd of caribou ran across the path of Peyton's party. The men ignored Peyton's advice and began shooting. As soon as the guns fired, they were surprised to see men, women, and children run from wigwams hidden among the trees along the lakeside. By the time Peyton arrived at the Indian village, all had left except three men, a woman, and a child. They too ran from the party, but the woman fell, delaying her long enough for them to catch up with and capture her. The child was carried off by one of the Beothuck men.

One of the three escaping Beothucks, possibly the husband of the Beothuck woman, came back and made peaceful gestures toward the party. He then tried to take the woman, but Peyton's men refused to release her. The Indian drew an axe, but dropped it after Peyton's men threatened him with their guns. At that time, two of the men started dragging the woman toward the wigwam.

Angered by this, the Beothuck rushed them, trying to rescue the woman. During the encounter, one of the men stabbed him with a bayonette; but that did not stop him. He took the bayonette from his attacker and, just as he was about to stab his assailant, Peyton drew his pistol and shot him.

The man he had killed was apparently the Beothuck chief, because when the other Beothucks saw this, they ran. Peyton took the woman, whose name was Demasduit, back to Twillingate and put her in the care of a missionary. She was given the English name Mary March, because she has been captured in the month of March. Several years later, she died aboard Captain Buchan's ship as he was attempting to reunite her with her people.

Jens Haven

Jens Haven is not a familiar name in Newfoundland history, but it should be. Haven, a Moravian missionary, was the first missionary to Labrador, and his good relationship with the Eskimos made possible the first treaty between the Eskimo and the English. The treaty brought some order to the Labrador coast, which was a lawless and dangerous frontier area at the time.

Haven, born in 1724 at Wust, Jutland, was a conceited and rough individual with an uncontrollable temper. He experienced a dramatic conversion to the Moravian faith after nearly being struck down by lightning. The event occurred during a raging thunder storm as Haven walked through a field. A shaft of lightning suddenly hit him. He thought it divine providence that he recovered and he prayed and wept day and night for a week, until he felt divine assurance of his salvation. In 1748 Jens Haven joined the Moravian Community and became a missionary.

An attempt by the Moravians to send four missionaries to Labrador in 1752 was forced back to Europe after the leader was murdered. Haven prayed hard and felt a strong urge to work among the Eskimos. He spent four years with the Eskimos of Greenland, where he experienced a series of dreams in which a voice called upon him to preach to those who had never heard the gospel.

These signs reassured his belief that God was calling him to Labrador. Governor Palliser of Newfoundland was delighted when Jens Haven arrived. Labrador was in a state of anarchy, the English were having trouble with the Eskimos, and fishing there was dangerous. Palliser wanted the Labrador coast made safe for the English and felt that missionaries could achieve this. In spite of the danger to his own life, Jens made his way into an Eskimo community and astonished them by speaking their language. He preached to them about respect for life and property, and pointed out the difference between the French and the English flags.

His reputation spread throughout Labrador and he became admired and respected by the Eskimos. Haven arranged to have the treaty signed between Governor Palliser and the Eskimos, but when he requested 100,000 acres of land for his church he was turned down because the Governor was not familiar with the Moravian religion. Jens Haven prayed for his church and was delighted by the way God answered his prayers. An Eskimo woman named Mikak was captured by the British and brought to England. She spoke so highly of Haven and his work that the English granted Haven's request for 100,000 acres in Labrador. Mikak and her husband, Tuglavino, accompanied Haven to a place called Eskimo Bay where the Moravians established their first mission. Jens Haven left Labrador at the age of 60 feeling old and weak. Shortly after that, he went blind. He passed away in 1796.

The Find at Port aux Choix

In 1967 Ted Farwell of Port aux Choix contracted with a bulldozer operator to dig out his backyard in order to lay the foundation for a theatre and poolhall extension. The excavation uncovered one of the most exciting archaeological finds in the history of North America.

The excavation revealed one hundred skeletons, mostly in kneeling positions. A team of archaeologists from Memorial University, lead by Dr. J. A. Tuck, set out for Port aux Choix to investigate the find. Their work began during the summer of 1968 and determined the site to be one of the most valuable Indian burial sites on this continent.

The MUN group found fifty-one burial mounds containing the remains of one hundred Indians. The Indians were of the Maritime Archaic culture, which had characterized the entire eastern seaboard from Maine to Labrador between 3,000 and 7,000 years ago. The skeletons were taken to MUN for study, where carbon dating and other scientific testing took place. The group determined the site had been used as an Indian burial ground for about 1,000 years, beginning well before 2000 B.C.

The one hundred skeletons at the site were found in typical red ochre burials, similar to those found in Asia and Europe dating back to the old Stone Age, 50,000 years ago.

Newfoundland author and historian, Harold Horwood suggested that it is possible that the Beothucks were the descendents of these ancient people. They had similar burial customs of red paint complex and the skeletons resembled those of the Beothuck.

Reverend Hollis Hiscock, an Anglican minister, shed some light on the reason for the skeletons being found in kneeling positions. He noted that when a member of a Dorset tribe was about to die, he was placed in an igloo. The igloo was immediately sealed, and the tribesman presumably died in a kneeling position.

Because of the discovery, Port aux Choix was designated a Canadian National Park in 1975, and a museum has been built on the site.

116

Chapter IX
SHIPWRECKS

Mutiny on the Diana
Lusitania
The Bell Island Ferry Tragedy
The Pollux and Truxton
Southern Cross
The Greenland Disaster
The Alice B. Marie
H. M. S. Sapphire
The Florizel
The Riverdale
The Wreck of the Evelyn
The Banshee
The Rescue of the Crew of the Heather
The Tolsby

117

Mutiny on the Diana

When the sealing ship *Diana* ran into trouble during the sealhunt of 1922, Captain John Parsons thought he could handle the crew and get the ship safely back to port. The last thing in the world he expected was a mutiny, — but that is what he got.

The *Diana* had 8,000 pelts on board when its propeller became damaged by a growler. Unable to move, the vessel became stuck in the ice. The moving tides forced the ice higher and higher until sheets of ice began moving in over the deck. The tremendous pressure from the ice forced the *Diana* up and out of the water, causing it to tip on its side, remaining on the ice.

Some of the crew, concerned that the *Diana* would sink, grabbed their belongings and got off. Captain Parsons did not share their concern. Although the ice had damaged the *Diana*, Parsons was sure that he could make the necessary repairs and keep her afloat. When the *Diana* was moved back into the water, word spread throughout the ship that it was badly leaking. The engines broke down, and the captain used pumps to keep her afloat and employed the sails for movement.

But the crew did not share the captain's confidence. Heavy winds were tossing the ship around, and further discontent spread when the men observed rats leaving the ship. The bad luck continued with the vessel crashing into an iceberg. The rigging became entangled in ice, and Jack Dodd, a crewmember, climbed up the yardarm and cut the lines, thereby freeing the *Diana*.

The crew requested Captain Parsons to send an S.O.S. and, when he refused, they threatened him with mutiny. Parsons sent the message, and the owners responded by sending the S.S. *Watchful*. While the captain and the owners felt the ship was in no real danger, the crew felt otherwise. They were convinced the ship was doomed and threatened to toss the captain overboard if he did not send another S.O.S.

On this occasion, Parsons pulled a gun and threatened to shoot the first man to approach him. When 40 crewmembers gathered together, Parsons rigged up a hose to give the mutineers a shot of steam if they made any attempt to overcome him.

The crew then left the ship, and the owners, after learning of the mutiny, gave up the *Diana* as lost. Orders were given to open the seacocks and allow the vessel to sink.

When the crew learned that the owners had given permission to the crew of the rescue ship *Sagona* to take the 8,000 pelts from the *Diana*, they set fire to it, causing it to sink. American writer George Allen England referred to this mutiny in his book *Vikings of the North*.

Lusitania

In the history of shipwrecks, the names *Titanic* and *Lusitania* loom larger than all others. They were both large liners and both sunk with great loss of life. Some readers however, may be surprised to learn that the *Lusitania*, with 436 people on board, went aground and sunk at Seal Cove near Renews on June 26, 1901. This *Lusitania* however, was not the same one which the German Navy torpedoed off Ireland during World War I; an attack which brought the United States into that war.

The *Lusitania* which sank at Seal Cove, was enroute from Liverpool, England to Montreal, with passengers mostly form Norway and Russia. The weather was excellent until the vessel neared Cape Race. The *Lusitania* was sailing at full speed when it became engulfed in fog. Captain William MacKay was not too concerned, because no land was in sight, and he kept the engines at full speed.

At 1:30 a.m. on June 26th, the people were thrown from their beds and others were knocked across hallways and rooms by a sudden jolt that vibrated through the whole ship. At first panic set in, because people thought that they had hit an iceberg. Mothers ran to the lifeboats carrying their children and wives clung to their husbands. A great relief spread over them when Captain MacKay advised them that they had struck land and not an iceberg.

The Captain and crew then began organizing an evacuation of the *Lusitania*.

When word of the grounding reached St. John's, people believed that because of the large number of passengers on the vessel there had been considerable loss of life. The *Ingraham*, *Glencoe* and *Algerine* immediately set out to pick up survivors. In just four hours everyone was removed safely from the *Lusitania* without any serious injury. There had been no loss of life.

The passengers were taken to St. John's and put up at the Prince's Rink, which was situated behind the site of the present Hotel Newfoundland; and at the old City Hall on Duckworth Street.

Arrangements were made and in a few days, the passengers were sent on to their destinations while the crew was returned to England.

Divers of Newfoundland might be interested in knowing that the *Lusitania* carried a large cargo of brandy and champagne.

The Bell Island Ferry Tragedy

The first fatality on the Bell Island ferry service was a major one. It occurred on the eve of November 11, 1940, just after darkness set in and a snowstorm began to develop. Twenty-four lives were lost when two passenger vessels, the *Garland* and the *Golden Dawn* collided just off shore from Bell Island.

The *Garland*, an eighteen ton vessel with a 44 horsepower diesel engine, was owned by Captain Norman Ash. It had left Portugal Cove at 5:30 p.m. with thirty persons on board, returning to Bell Island. As the *Garland* moved out of the Cove, the *Golden Dawn* was preparing to leave Bell Island to bring passengers to Portugal Cove. The *Golden Dawn* was also a diesel vessel, weighing fourteen tons. At 5:45 p.m. the *Golden Dawn* moved away from the Bell Island wharf. It was a dark snowy evening and Captain Mitchell noticed a bright light moving towards his ship, but could not make out what it was. While he was attempting to avoid collision, a snow squall came up. Just as it cleared, the *Garland* suddenly appeared on the starboard side of the *Golden Dawn*. It was too late to avoid disaster. Both vessels were travelling at full-throttle when the collision occurred.

A police constable on the wharf heard a terrific crash, followed by terrifying screams. Within five minutes, the *Garland* went to the bottom, about a quarter mile from the wharf.

Captain Mitchell tried unsuccessfully to start the engines of the *Golden Dawn*, and it drifted about a mile away from the crash scene. The engineer on the *Golden Dawn* set fire to his coat, and the flames attracted rescuers.

Rescue vessels set out from Bell Island after word of the tragedy spread, and the first to reach the scene were Fred Snow and Fred Ralph. They rescued Captain Ash, and three passengers of the *Garland*. The survivors had clung to an oil barrel that had floated off the deck of the vessel as she sunk. Most of those who died were killed by the tremendous impact of the collision. Rescue efforts were called off at 2 a.m. but resumed again at dawn under the direction of Head Constable Russell and several CID officers. Seventeen vessels were used in the search and twenty-one bodies were recovered.

The ferry terminal at Portugal Cove where the ferry Garland departed for the last time on November 11th, 1940.

Photo — Jack Fitzgerald

The Pollux and Truxton

There is a hospital at St. Lawrence that was a gift from the President of the United States to the people of that area, in appreciation of their courage and valiant effort in rescuing and caring for, 168 survivors of the *Pollux* and *Truxton* disasters of 1942.

The tragedy took place during February of 1942, when a convoy bringing supplies to Argentia Base ran into a very severe winter storm near Lawn. The supply ship *U.S.S. Pollux* and the destroyer *U.S.S. Truxton* were part of that convoy.

The storm drove the *Truxton* and the *Pollux* off course; and at 4:30 a.m. on February 18, the *Pollux* went ashore near Lawn. The area is surrounded by sheer clifts and the sailors found themselves trapped. The ship was also threatening to break up under the constant beatings of the weather.

Rescue teams from Lawn were sent out to the disaster area, and, in spite of the raging storm and dangerous clifts, began the hazardous rescue operation. They managed to save about eighty men, but the ship broke in two and the others went down with it.

Meanwhile, the *Truxton* became separated from the convoy and was driven northward by the storm. At 5:30 a.m. the captain put the engines in reverse because he thought he was about to hit and iceberg. There was no iceberg but the ship grounded on a large reef, two hundred yards from Chambers Cove.

When word of this disaster reached St. Lawrence, the mines were closed and the men organized rescue parties. The *Truxton* split in two, but half of it remained afloat. The rescuers managed to save the others. The military sent out naval rescue units. 168 people were rescued, and 204 drowned in the two disasters. Ninety men were buried at St. Lawrence, but their bodies were returned to the United States for burial in 1945.

In appreciation for their heroism and unselfish sharing of goods to the needy, the U.S. Government decided to build a hospital at St. Lawrence. That hospital opened during June 1954, and a plaque from the U. S. President can be seen on its walls.

Southern Cross

The greatest single disaster in a spring of tragedies and the most puzzling in the long history of the Newfoundland seal fishery was the loss of the ill-fated *Southern Cross*.

For more than 70 years, the fate of the *Southern Cross* has been a secret locked somewhere at the bottom of the Atlantic. This ship, with 173 on board, disappeared while returning from the seal hunt in the Gulf of St. Lawrence, sometime between March 31 and April 2, 1914.

On March 12, Captain John Clarke, had sailed for the Gulf with a crew of 173. Other sealing ships departing the same day included the *Terra Nova*, *Neptune*, *Eric*, and the *Viking*. The *Southern Cross* was not equipped with wireless; information regarding her progress was received indirectly, through reports sent in by other ships. There was no direct contact between the *Southern Cross* and land until March 30th when a message was received in St. John's reading: 'Last evening matters were astir in sealing circles when the news was currently reported that a steamer had passed out of the gulf loaded.'

The arrival of a sealing steamer in St. John's was a major attraction at that time, and at around 6:30 p.m., the day after word had been received that a sealing vessel was returning, a crowd gathered near the general post office on Water Street to get the latest seal hunt information.

Many conflicting messages were posted as to what steamer was coming. The first reports were uncertain as to whether the vessel leaving the gulf had been the *Terra Nova* or the *Southern Cross*. The first indications that the ship was in trouble came on Tuesday, March 31. A message read: 'The *Southern Cross* had not reported since passing St. Pierre, yesterday afternoon, and the general opinion is that she is to heave to in Placentia Bay. It was a fine night and she likely passed St. Lawrence and Burin.'

Another message reported the *Southern Cross* was heavily laden and could travel at only 5 knots. When a sudden storm struck, experienced mariners speculated she would lay anchor at St. Mary's Bay, as she had last been seen fifteen or twenty miles from there.

On April 1, Captain Connors of the *Portia* cabled Bowrings to report he had sighted the *Southern Cross* five miles west northwest of Cape Pine at 11 a.m. on the previous day. He speculated she went to North Harbour, St. Mary's Bay. That was the last anyone ever saw of the *Southern Cross*.

The Cape Race wireless operator reported she had not passed Cape Race or Trepassey. A search by the *Kyle* and the *Senneca*, a U.S. patrol vessel, failed to turn up any sign of the missing steamer. Experienced sealers speculated the *Southern Cross*, hindered by an excessive cargo and caught up in a bad storm, was shipwrecked and went to the bottom of the Atlantic. A replica of the Southern Cross was constructed years later by Osmond White of Blackmarsh Road, and sold to Gerald S. Doyle, a noted collector of such models.

The Greenland Disaster

There were many disasters at the Newfoundland seal hunt, but three of the greatest were: the *Newfoundland*, the *Viking*, and the *Greenland* disasters. In this story, I will deal with the famous *Greenland* disaster. First news of that tragedy did not reach St. John's until a week after it occurred because there were no wireless sets on the ships. The story had its beginning on Monday, March 21, 1891 with the *Greenland* picking up pelts 70 miles north of the Funk Islands. The sealers on the *Greenland* had killed enough seals to fill the ship, but their catch was plundered by other sealers.

Captain George Barbour ordered his men back onto the ice to make good the loss. It was a fine morning, and the ship sailed northward, dropping four watch groups on the way. Barbour then returned by the same route, picking up the seals.

At 6 p.m. a windstorm suddenly erupted, accompanied by blinding snow squalls. The first watch managed to get on board, but then things began to go wrong. The *Greenland* became trapped in ice. As darkness set in, temperatures dropped and the intensity of the storm grew. There were few seals killed that day which meant there was little fat available for the men to build fires. To keep their blood circulating, the men walked all night long. But the blizzard continued all through the next day. Some men wandered away from the group, and were never seen again.

When darkness descended the second night, the storm began to abate. The survivors could hear the continual blowing of the ship's whistle. At dawn the next morning the storm was over and the ice opened up, freeing the *Greenland*. When the vessel arrived at the place where the men had been stranded, they found only six survivors of the 54 who had been lost in the storm. They found 24 bodies which they stripped down and packed in ice for transportation back to St. John's. Nearly four days later, the *Greenland* arrived at Bay de Verde and sent word of the disaster to the capital city.

Thousands lined the waterfront the next day to view the arrival of the *Greenland* carrying the victims and survivors of the great tragedy. The bodies were dug from the ice, wrapped in quilts, and taken to the Seaman's Home on Duckworth Street. A total of 48 men perished in the *Greenland* disaster.

The Alice B. Marie

The story of the wreck of the *Alice B. Marie* off the coast of Clam Cove, near Cape Race, is worth telling because of an unusual occurrence that took place at the time. During September 1877, the vessel was on its way to St. Pierre from Cadiz with a cargo of salt on board. After 42 days at sea it ran into heavy seas and hurricane-force winds near Cape Race. There were seven men and a young boy on board the small vessel. The storm made it impossible to navigate and the Alice B. Marie washed closer and closer to the ragged-edged clifts of Clam Cove.

In a final effort to avoid disaster, the captain ordered the men to take in the top-gallant sail and roll down the topsails. The peak of the mainsail was hoisted and all the sails were trimmed, but to no avail. When the lookout cried "We're on the rocks!", the captain and crew were still working to save the ship. Suddenly, a raging surf tossed the *Alice B. Marie* between the beach and the clifts. Two men made an attempt to take a lifeline to shore, using one of the dories, but a wave took them away and they disappeared into the deep. By this time, spectators had gathered on shore, but due to the severity of the storm, they were unable to do anything except pray.

Then, a gigantic wave seemed to build out of nowhere and washed over the men and the ship, smashing the vessel into several pieces. Both the men and the ship disappeared. The crowd on shore stared in disbelief and shock. When it seemed to be all over and there was no sign of any survivors, the crowd began to walk away.

Then someone spotted something moving on the beach! Everyone ran towards the object. It was the fifteen-year-old cabin boy from the *Alice B. Marie*, Henry Ria. Witnesses described the event as a miracle. The distance, combined with the raging seas made it impossible for anyone to swim to shore. The boy was saved because the wave that broke up the ship had tossed him towards the shore and safety.

H. M. S. Sapphire

During the early 1970's, members of the Newfoundland Archaeology Society recovered hundreds of artifacts from the *H. M. S. Sapphire*, which had been sunk during the battle at Bay Bulls on September 11, 1696. The discovery of the wreck of the *Sapphire* is an important event because it represents the oldest identified vessel to have sunk by the French in Newfoundland waters.

Built in 1675, the *Sapphire* was a 32-gun frigate under the command of Captain Thomas Cleasby and used as a patrol and escort vessel during the King William and Mary War that raged from 1689 to 1698. Because of the threat to the British fishing and supply vessels crossing the Atlantic it was necessary for the ships to move in convoy with a naval escort. Bay Bulls became the centre for convoy operations in Newfoundland.

The *Sapphire* was in port at Bay Bulls preparing to escort fishing vessels back to England when a French squadron appeared on the scene. The French squadron consisted of nine man-o-wars commanded by the Governor of Placentia, Monsieur de Borouillas.

The French squadron entered Bay Bulls, destroying several shore batteries and it moved towards the *Sapphire*. Captain Cleasby, realizing he could not win a battle with the French decided to scuttle and burn the ship to prevent the French from taking possession of it. Cleasby and the crew tried to escape overland to Ferryland; were captured and taken to France; and eventually released to the British in a prisoner exchange. Captain Cleasby was court martialed, but was vindicated and given a new command.

Almost 281 years to the day, the *Sapphire* was rediscovered by divers at the bottom of Bay Bulls Harbour.

Faculty members of the Engineering Department at Memorial University used an air lift to remove the heavy layers of silt that covered the *Sapphire*. The exposed artifacts were then put into special containers. The compressor providing air for the lift was kept on a large raft moored over the wreck. To preserve the historic site, the Provincial Government declared the site a protected historic area in 1975.

The find of the *Sapphire* has been one of the most important marine historical discoveries of this century.

The Florizel

The *Florizel*, with 138 people on board, set out from St. John's at 8 p.m. on Saturday, February 23, 1918. She was heading for New York carrying a quarter of a million dollars worth of fish products. The *Florizel* was equipped with wireless, and her captain, William Martin, was a veteran of the sea and considered to be one of the most careful navigators sailing from Newfoundland.

Less than an hour out at sea, a southeast gale sprang up, with a thick snow, and it blew with great force until midnight. Then it suddenly veered to east north east, blowing just as strongly until 4 a.m. the next day, when the snow changed to rain.

The steamer struck a reef, about 250 yards offshore from Horn Head near Cappahayden, on the Southern Shore. It soon began to break up under the pounding of the seas. The first news of the stranding reached St. John's shortly before 6 a.m. in the terse message from the ill-fate steamer picked up by the Admiralty wireless station at Mount Pearl: 'S.O.S. FLORIZEL ASHORE NEAR CAPE RACE. FAST GOING TO PIECES.'

Immediate preparations were made to send help. A number of ships responded to the S.O.S. and sailed out of St. John's to go to the *Florizel*'s rescue. A special train was prepared and stocked with needed supplies and help including: doctors, nurses, and police. It was dispatched from St. John's on the Trepassey Branch Line.

When people from communities near the wreck arrived at Horn Head on Sunday morning, their first thought was that there was no one alive. A tremendous sea was running on the exposed shore. Its force was so strong that it had torn away most of the superstructure. The ship's tall funnel towered above the wreck like a tombstone. Most of those already dead had been drowned in their berths below deck, or swept away with the superstructure when they ran topside trying to escape. The various rescue ships had to proceed with caution to avoid being wrecked themselves.

By ship and train, the survivors, injured, frost-bitten, harrowed, but glad to be alive, were brought back to St. John's. Many of the bodies were recovered from the breakers or found in the landwash and were taken to St. John's for burial. The deathtoll was great. A total of 94, including many prominent Newfoundlanders, lost their lives in the *Florizel* disaster.

The Peter Pan monument at Bowring Park was erected by Sir Edgar Bowring in memory of his god child Betty Munn who died in the Florizel disaster. The monument was unveiled on August 29, 1925.
Photo — Wayne Madden

The Riverdale

Sixteen men and a young boy set out from Channel, Port aux Basques on October 8, 1871 as crew of the *Riverdale* When she was towed into Halifax harbour a week later, only three people were still alive.

On the fifth day at sea, the vessel had run into a hurricane gale that had tossed her on her beam, beginning a 72 hour ordeal and battle for the survival of her crew. Edward Genge was the first to drown. He died when his cabin quickly filled with water. Genge's body remained there until it was removed after the ship had been towed to Halifax harbour.

When the heavy wind tipped the ship, the spars were all washed overboard, and the *Riverdale* jetted through the water for about 15 minutes in the tipped position, and then turned upright. Captain Philip Blackmore and Benjamin Buffett had both been washed overboard. Buffett drowned, but Blackmore managed to grab hold of one of the spars being dragged by the vessel.

Meanwhile, the mate, two seamen and the boy, lashed themselves as best they could, to the deck railings. The first night was a terrible one for them. They had no food and very little clothing; and the heavy seas kept rolling in over them. Dawn brought no hope for them. Although the storm was over, the seas ran high and it seemed the wreck could not stay afloat much longer. Terrible pangs of hunger and thirst tormented the men. The boy died and his body was washed away. The hope of the surviving men rose when a vessel came near, but it passed them by. Some saltfish broke away from the cargo deck, but the men would not eat it, knowing it would only cause intense, burning thirst.

The Captain clung to the dragging spar as long as he could, but after being exposed to the cold, heavy seas and hunger, he died and slipped into the sea. Finally, when the sea became calm, the surviving three men loosened the lashings from their arms and legs and exercised to gain relief for their numbed limbs.

Twenty miles southwest of the Sambro Islands they were rescued by the *Veruna*. A line was put aboard the *Riverdale* and she was towed into Halifax. The rescued men were later reunited with their families at Channel, Port aux Basques.

The Wreck of the Evelyn

On January 10, 1913, during a blinding snowstorm, the *Evelyn*, travelling from the West Indies with only sand ballast aboard, was wrecked on the north side of the Isle aux Bois while attempting to seek shelter in Ferryland Harbour.

Captain Edgar Burke and his crew of six men were rescued by a group of men from Ferryland: Jim, Bill, and Jack Barnable, and their brother-in-law, Will Furlong, along with Howard Morry and two Devereaux brothers, Mike and Johnny.

Noticing the distressed ship through a break in the drifting snow, the men launched a skiff and braving the storming seas which at times threatened to swamp their boat, they somehow managed to land on the opposite side of the island.

Scaling the icy cliffs, they crossed over the island to where the crew were stranded on the rocks below. Failing to lower a rope, due to the high winds; the slightest member of the group, Will Furlong, was lowered down over the cliffs and one by one, each man was pulled to safety.

Their next task was to get the crew and themselves safely back to shore; for a plank had been damaged when their skiff was thrown against the rocks. They managed to keep the water bailed out as they desperately rowed back to shore.

The captain and the crew were provided with food and shelter in the homes of William Bryan and Matthew Barnable and were taken from there to St. John's the following day by horse and slide.

(Compliments Ferryland Museum)

131

The Banshee

One of the ships which passed over the waters where the ill-fated *Titanic* had gone down a day or so earlier, was a Newfoundland vessel named the *Banshee*.

The *Banshee* first came to Newfoundland waters during January 1905, when she was chartered to replace the *Harold* to carry fish from McRae's, at Harbour Grace, to European markets.

In an interview following the arrival in port of the *Banshee*, its captain, Robert Willis, said that they passed near the *Titanic* disaster in one of the most harrowing experiences he had ever encountered while at sea.

Willis said it happened on a trip from Cadiz to St. John's on the morning of May 14, 1912. The *Banshee*'s crew saw floating debris in the waters; including a wardrobe with brass knobs, a part of a cabin door, and a piece of rail.

Shortly after that, they viewed the bodies of two men floating face-down in the water. At this stage, Willis and his crew had not heard anything about the *Titanic* disaster, and they were puzzled by their sightings.

Upon arrival in St. John's, they learned that what they had seen was some of the wreckage of the *Titanic*. During the same voyage, about 120 miles south of Cape Race, the *Banshee* crewmembers sighted a dirigible. The sack of the balloon was inflated and it was of a large size.

The crew investigated, but saw no sign of life. They had no means of taking the object to port, so they continued to St. John's, hoping to find out what had happened. Many efforts were made to identify the dirigible, but they all failed.

The Rescue of the Crew of the Heather

A serious error in judgement resulted in the Captain and crew of a Newfoundland cargo ship having a close brush with death and several days of hardship, hunger and exposure at sea.

The *Heather* was returning to St. John's from a foreign voyage during March of 1856 when she became jammed in the ice. Four of the crew members abandoned the ship against Captain Richard Ash's wishes because they feared the ship would be crushed. Their concerns were certainly justified. A short while later, the ice began carrying the vessel onto the rocks. The captain and the remainder of his crew then abandoned ship, minutes before she hit the clifts. The vessel did not sink, however; but the ice had broken up and they were unable to get back to her. On individual pans of ice,the three crew members and Captain Ash drifted south during the night and all the next day. As nightfall approached, they were without shelter or food and the weather was beginning to worsen.

They had drifted as far south as Ferryland and prayed that someone in that area would spot them before they drifted out to sea. Fortunately for them, a Mrs. Carter in Ferryland looked through her window and noticed them drifting by on an ice floe. She advised Father Murphy, the parish priest, and a rescue attempt was organized.

The rescue team was made up of ten brave Ferryland men. They included Francis Geary, John Costello, William Morry, Marmaduke Clowe, Henry Morry, Richard Sullivan, Thomas Moore, James Sweeney, Peter Kelly, and John O'Keefe. The rescue team picked up the stranded men from the pan of ice nearest shore first and returned them to Ferryland.

Upon returning to rescue Captain Ash and the others, the rescuers themselves found their lives in danger. Just after removing the captain and his men from the ice pan, a storm broke and strong winds forced their boat out to sea, to the horror of their families and friends watching from shore.

By the time the storm had subsided the men had drifted forty miles out to sea. When the storm ended, they managed to bring their boat into Witless Bay. Captain Ash had suffered a great deal from exposure and had to be taken to St. John's for medical treatment. Thanks to the heroism of the Ferryland ten, no lives were lost.

The Tolsby

When the twenty-five-man crew of the *Tolsby* set sail from Galveston, Texas on December 27, 1907 for France, not one of those aboard had heard of a community in Newfoundland known as 'the Drooks'. Two weeks later, they owed their lives to a group of fishermen from the Drooks, a community near Trepassey on the Southern Shore.

On January 13 the *Tolsby* was in the middle of a blinding snowstorm. Captain C. J. Payne heard the whistle blowing at Power's head, but not knowing anything about a navigational aid in that area, other than the one at Cape Race, figured his ship was a safe distance from the shore. Payne and his crew were totally surprised when the vessel crashed upon the rocks at Little Seal Cove.

The vessel was near enough to shore for the men to see the 500 foot clift jutting up steeply from the beach. Captain Payne decided that the men would be safer if they remained on the *Tolsby*, but the storm worsened, and the pounding surf began tearing the ship apart. the lifeboats were lowered, but also broke up in the water; only one, with five men, made it to shore.

When the vessel began to break up, the others jumped into the water and swam for shore. It was only a short swim, and they all made it to safety. The twenty-five men were then stranded on a strip of shore in the cove between the raging sea and the cliff.

As dawn broke, the men were ready to give up, when ropes suddenly appeared down the clift as if coming out of nowhere. It was Joe Perry, leading a band of fishermen from the Drooks. Perry put a rope around his own waist and descended the precipice. As he descended, he cleared large rocks away to make the rescue easier.

One by one the stranded men were rescued. The men were given warm clothing and food by the Drooks' inhabitants, and before heading out for St. John's, the *Tolsby* crew took up a collection among themselves to give Perry and his men as a token of their appreciation for their outstanding heroism and fine hospitality.

Chapter X
WARS

It may not be surprising to read of Newfoundlander's involvement in World Wars I and II but most people will be fascinated to learn of Newfoundlanders being involved in the Boer War, the Spanish-American War, the Mexican Revolution, the U.S. Civil War, the American War of Independence and the Crimean War. This chapter chronicles some of these stories, including some fascinating tales from World Wars I and II. Many others I have broadcast on *Notebook* will be included in future publications.

A Newfoundlander at the Spanish American War
Captain Jack Randell
Newfoundland Mercenaries
The Founder of Mount Pearl
The Queen of St. George's
Foul Weather Jack
The Siege of Sebastopol
German U-Boat Surrenders
The Nazi Prison Camp in Newfoundland
Beaumont Hamel
Gas-Mask Inventor

A Newfoundlander
at the Spanish American War

Newfoundlanders have traveled the four corners of the earth and their deeds, achievements, and adventures would make a history in itself. The story of John Cooper of Trinity Bay is but one of these stories.

Cooper moved to New York from Trinity and following a brief stint as a fisherman joined the Fifteenth New York Infantry Regiment. On May 1, 1898, young Cooper was on his way to Virginia to join the expeditionary force going to Cuba to take part in the Spanish-American War. That war, one of the shortest in world history, started April 21 and was over three and a half months later, on August 12. Most of the military activity was confined to Cuba and the Phillipines.

The Spanish Army held two strong points in Cuba: the village of El Caney and the hill of San Juan. Cooper was in the thick of both battles and was at the front with troops making a major assault at Fort Santiago. The fighting was heavy and the Americans suffered many casualties.

A soldier near Cooper carrying the Stars and Stripes was shot and killed. As he fell, Cooper grabbed the American flag before it hit the ground.

Surrounded by heavy gunfire, Cooper fought his way courageously up the slope and managed to plant the flag at the top of the Spanish Fort. Spurred on by Cooper's display of courage, the Americans went on to win the Battle at Santiago and the Spanish-American War.

John Cooper was later awarded a medal for bravery by the U. S. Government. After receiving the honour, Cooper returned home to Trinity Bay for a six-week vacation.

Captain Jack Randell

A Newfoundlander who fought in several wars, skippered an Arctic expedition and was decorated by the King of England, once had his ship shot out from under him by the U.S. Coast Guard. This man, Captain Jack Randell, who led a life full of adventure, was born at Port Rexton, then known as Ship Cove, in 1879.

Randell's love for adventure lead him to the Royal Navy and the Boer War in South Africa. He was only 20 years old at the time, and was assigned as an artilleryman with the Canadian Field Artillery. When Canadian Forces pulled out of Africa, he voluntarily signed up with Howard's Canadian Scouts and stayed at the war zone until the war ended.

Upon his return to Newfoundland, he was presented with several medals for courage by the Duchess of York and her husband, who later became King George V of England.

By the time Randell was 28 years old, he had earned his deep water master's ticket for any tonnage vessel on any ocean, steam or sail. Captain Randell was a rough and ready type of individual who even fought professional fighters in clubs to raise money for food. Widespread malaria and sleeping black water diseases did not discourage Randell from taking an assignment on a dredger on the west coast of Africa.

Captain Randell built a good reputation as a reliable skipper and was called upon frequently by the British to deliver vessels all over the world. He was highly regarded by Lloyd's of London, and once saved them thousands of dollars by salvaging a grounded dredger.

His good relationship with the British led to his being appointed to deliver a new dredger to Imperial Russia, an assignment that brought him into German-Russian espionage. A German agent had stolen the blueprints of a Russian Naval base and was on his way out of the country on Randell's boat, carrying the top secret documents. Randell got him into a drinking contest and kept him drinking long enough for the Russian agents to catch up and make an arrest. World War I broke out shortly afterward, and Randell skippered armed trawlers, minesweepers, and subchasers. His performance in that war earned him a Distinguished Service Cross from King George V and the unofficial title 'Pirate of the Grand Fleet'. He retired from the Royal Navy as Lieutenant Commander.

During prohibition years, he turned to the profitable rum-running business, and was doing well on his vessel the *I'm Alone*, until the U.S. Coast Guard blasted it out of the water and sent Randell to jail.

Capt. Jack Randell

Newfoundland Mercenaries

Jim Baird and Patrick Sweeney of St. John's were killed during a wartime conflict and their two Newfoundland companions Harry Carter and Robert Mugford were wounded. However, it was neither the First nor Second World War, nor any of the many wars so famous in our British history. These four Newfoundland adventurers had gotten tied up on the rebel side of the Mexican Revolution of 1911 and met their Waterloo at the Battle of Casas Grandes.

The four Newfoundlanders had been attracted to the Rebel Mexican Army by the offer of $300 per month and a promise of five thousand acres of land when the government of Porfirio Diez was defeated and replaced by rebel leaders. The leader of the rebel forces was Francisco Madero, who had been defeated by Diez in the presidential election of 1910. Following that election, Diez ordered the arrest and imprisonment of Madero. When Madero finally got out of prison, he started the revolution that ousted Diez, and Madero himself became president.

Most of Madero's forces were mercenaries who had fought in conflicts all over the world. When things got rough at the Battle of Casas Grandes, the inexperienced Mexicans left the battlefield. The others, including the four Newfoundlanders, fought to within forty feet of the federal forces using dynamite and nitroglycerine. The attack came to a stop when a bullet hit a 100-pound package of dynamite in the saddlebags of the rebel Captain. Captain Lloyd, born in Scotland, had lived for some years in Newfoundland before becoming a soldier of fortune.

Baird and Sweeney were killed and Mugford and Carter injured in the blast. The famous battle lasted only 90 minutes with Madero's forces being defeated. Carter and Mugford were carried to safety from the battlefield by their comrades. Although the rebels lost that battle, they eventually won the war, and Madero became president. The new president however reneged on his promise of land grants to the Mexicans and mercenaries.

Mugford left Mexico for the U. S. but Carter enlisted in the forces of Pancho Villa. He was with Villa while Villa was being hounded by the great U. S. World War I hero, General John J. Pershing. Carter eventually left Villa's forces and again settled down in Mexico City.

The Founder of Mount Pearl

Mount Pearl had its beginning with the arrival in Newfoundland of a famous British navel hero, Sir James Pearl, who at first called the area 'Mount Cochrane' after the Governor of Newfoundland at the time. Pearl was born at Yarmouth, N.S.

in 1789, had joined the British Navy at the age of eleven. At fifteen he was a midshipman and then an officer on the 98-gun British warship *Neptune*.

In this capacity he fought valiantly in the Battle of Trafalgar. By the time Pearl was eighteen years old, he was a lieutenant in the British Navy. He was one of the volunteer officers who led the Battle which destroyed the French fleet at the Basques Roads. During this battle, Pearl was seriously wounded and was actually blown right off his ship, the *Mediator*.

Pearl distinguished himself in many naval battles. In the Burmese War he commanded 500 boats and 30 transport ships and once rescued 200 Chinese after their ship broke up and sank.

The founder of Mount Pearl received a host of honours in recognition of his bravery and military achievements. The British Patriotic Fund presented him with a sword; the King of the Netherlands presented him with a gold medal; and British merchants at Canton presented him with a plaque in honour of his rescuing the 200 Chinese sailors. The plaque displayed the inscription: 'By that act he exalted the British character among the Chinese'. He was knighted in 1836.

Pearl retired from service in 1827, having reached the level of Commander. He arrived in Newfoundland in 1829 with a grant from the British Government for one thousand acres of land. He presented the order to Governor Cochrane and selected 1,000 acres in the area now known as Mount Pearl. However, when he tried to survey the land, the Governor received petitions from local residents with applications for the Crown land in the same area. Because of this, the Governor would only permit Pearl to take 500 acres in that area. Sir James Pearl reluctantly agreed to seek the remaining 500 acres in another area. He named his estate 'Mount Cochrane', in honour of the Governor. Pearl used his own money to build a public road through his property.

Pearl is also considered one of the fathers of Responsible Government. In 1839 he took petitions to London requesting Responsible Government and presented them personally to King William.

Pearl died on January 13, 1840 and was buried at the old Church of England cemetery near the Courthouse on Duckworth Street. There is a plaque erected to the memory of Pearl at the County Court House in Yarmouth, Nova Scotia where he was born.

The Queen of St. George's

Ann Hulan, was known as the Queen of St. George's Bay during the early nineteenth century. Ann was a courageous and spirited leader who founded one of the first and largest farms on Newfoundland's west coast. When William Epps Cormack made his historical walk across Newfoundland in 1822, he was welcomed as a guest at Ann Hulan's farm.

In addition to operating a large farm, Ann Hulan owned a small cargo ship named the *Industry*. It was not uncommon for her to take her place among the ship's crew on one of its cargo-carrying assignments. One such escapade of Ann's developed into an international incident.

During that period, many American ships had been captured by British naval forces and brought to St. John's. This brought many American privateers to Newfoundland and Canadian waters to get revenge and capture some ships of their own. It was into this set of circumstances that Ann Hulan's *Industry*, sailed during August 1812, under Captain Clement Renouf.

As the vessel neared St. Mary's Bay it was intercepted by a Yankee privateer, the *Benjamin Franklin*, under the command of Captain Josiah Ingersoll.

A prize crew took over Hulan's ship and sailed it to New York. Because the *Industry* was a small cargo vessel and not part of any military action, U. S. authorities were not certain as to what to do with that vessel. The U. S. Government set up a Court of Enquiry and Nathanial Davis was appointed to conduct it. Ann Hulan appeared before the Commission and obviously made a good impression on Davis.

When the enquiry concluded, Davis wrote U. S. President James Monroe recommending the the *Industry* be looked upon as an object of charity rather than a prisoner of war. President Monroe granted a release but because captured vessels during wartime could not be released, it was put up on public auction.

The Americans arranged for Ann Hulan to be the only bidder at the auction and she got her property back for a token one dollar yankee bill.

Ann Hulan and her crew were back in St. George's in time to celebrate the Christmas of 1812.

Foul Weather Jack

The nickname 'Foul Weather Jack' is known the world over and is associated with persons who seem to attract bad luck wherever they go. The name originated as a nickname for John Byron, who served as Governor of Newfoundland from 1769 to 1772. During the American War of Independence, Byron was Vice-Admiral of the British Navy. In this capacity he led a squadron of warships to relieve the British forces in North America. Byron's force encountered one of the worst sea storms on record and his fleet was scattered. This weakened the British forces, contributing to their loss of the war. A short while after that, he did battle with Count d'Estaing of Granada, but the outcome of that battle was inconclusive.

Byron began his military career at the age of eighteen in 1740 as a midshipman in in the British Navy. His ship was lost on the coast of Chile where he and the other crewmembers were taken prisoners by an Indian tribe and forced to work as servants to Indian families. An Indian girl became infatuated with Byron and this made his term of enslavement to the Indians much easier.

The girl brought him extra food and he was treated a little better than the other captives. Eventually, the Englishmen were released, and, by 1745, Byron was back in England, where he wrote a book dealing with his adventures on the coast of Chili.

John Byron was the grandfather of the world-famous poet Lord George Byron. This poet was so impressed by his grandfather's narrative that he used it as the basis for the ship-wreck scene in Don Juan.

John Byron was made a naval commander and was sent on an exploration expedition to the South Seas. but once more he met failure. The only thing he discovered was that Captain Cook had been there ahead of him.

In 1769, he was appointed Governor of Newfoundland. While governor, he had his portrait painted by Sir Joshua Reynolds. During the 1970s, this portrait, now more than 200 years old, fetched $15,000 at an art auction at Sotheby's Art Gallery in London. the famous painting, and the nickname 'Foul Weather Jack' are all that is left of the legacy of Newfoundland's Governor John Byron.

The Siege of Sebastopol

The Siege of Sebastopol is a military battle that may now be remembered only by the most avid students of world history. However, that battle was the major one of the Crimean War, fought between 1883 and 1856. That war saw France, England, and Italy align with Turkey in defeating Russia.

The French upheld the honour of their national flag in the celebrated capture of Malakoff and the first man to ascend the heights there was Lieutenant McMahon, who later became the Duke of Magenta, and later president of the French Republic.

A similar great honour was won by the British at the siege of Sebastopol. In this case however, it was a man named Robbins from Lower Island Cove who was the first man to scale the walls at Sebastopol. When Robbins reached the top of the wall, the first thing he did was to shout: "Three cheers for Newfoundland!" The British officer who came after him shouted "Three cheers for England!"

Robbins was well equipped to scale high walls. As a matter of fact, most men from Lower Island Cove had a reputation for climbing high cliffs. They had been brought up to it from their earliest days to climb the cliffs of Baccalieu Island in search of birds' eggs. It was there that young Robbins got the real training that enabled him to race his fellow soldiers up the walls at Sebastopol.

Two other Newfoundlanders took part in the battle at Sebastopol: they were Captain James Stanton of St. John's and John Bully Ayre. Both men were on the H.M.S. Terrible. They were also at the Battle of Odessa where John Ayre was awarded a medal for his heroism.

Newfoundlanders' daring, heroism, and love of adventure has brought them to all parts of the world and has created an interesting aspect of our history that has yet to be written.

German U-Boat Surrenders

During May 1945, the German U-Boat U-190 surrendered and was brought to Bay Bulls Harbour. She was supposed to have surrendered at Halifax, but was brought to Bay Bulls because of hostile feelings at Halifax.

The hostility resulted from the sinking of the Royal Canadian Fleet minesweeper *Esquimalt* by the U-190 a month earlier, causing the loss of 22 lives. One of those lost was Chesley Shave of St. John's. British sources claimed the U-190 had actually surrendered at Halifax, but, because of hostile feeling in the area, she was taken to Bay Bulls.

A British sailor holds the White Ensign and the Sivastikia on board the captured German U-Boat 190 at Bay Bulls.

Courtesy — Provincial Archives, Nfld.

The U-190, commanded at that time by Hans Edwin Reith surrendered on the night of May 10, 1945 to Commanding Officer of the *HMS Victoriaville*, Newfoundland-born Lieutenant Commander Lester Hickey of St. Jacques. Hickey received his early education in St. John's, where he resided with his grandmother on Fleming Street. Hickey had a distinguished military career, being mentioned in dispatches on June 2, 1943 for outstanding performance during the Battle of the North Atlantic. He was also awarded the Order of the British Empire. The U-190 was the first of the German U-boats to enter a Newfoundland port with the black flag flying in token of surrender and the white ensign gaily fluttering from the gaff.

The Germans were taken aboard Hickey's ship and interrogated. Hundreds of spectators watched from shore and the press seemed to be everywhere. The German prisoners were a motley crew and it was evident that they had not had a haircut of a shave for a long time. Although their faces had a pasty look, they appeared to have been well-fed. The majority wore blue rubberized coats. One of the men wore the German Iron Cross.

The Germans smiled and began jesting in their own language, but that quickly stopped when they noticed the unsmiling faces of the Canadian ratings gazing at them.

The sub itself looked like a huge unmarked floating log. It was 200 feet long, with a 500 ton capacity and was one of the larger and best-equipped German subs. The U-190 carried a crew of 49; 22 torpedoes and 42 mines. Up to the time of surrender, she had sunk the British Merchant ship *Empire Lakehead* which had been sailing in convoy from Sydney, N. S. to England.

The 65 crewmembers on board were all lost in that attack. Her only other victim was the *Esquimalt*.

The U-190's periscope was preserved and is on display at the Crow's Nest, an officers' club near the War Memorial in St. John's.

The Nazi Prison Camp in Newfoundland

In 1985, Penni Clarke, a grade eleven student at Victoria, Conception Bay, completed a research assignment as a school project. The paper she presented to her teacher represented an outstanding piece of research, and in addition to that brought to light a detailed account of an historic happening at Victoria which had been forgotten. Thanks to Penni Clarke and the Newfoundland Historic Society, I am able to present you with the story of the proposed Nazi Interment Camp at Victoria.

At the beginning of the Second World War, the British were rounding up and arresting all citizens of German origin. In less than two months they had ten thousand people in custody, creating a major problem as to what to do with them. Arrangements were made to transport them to prisons in Canada and Australia. Discussions with the Newfoundland Government led to a decision on June 14, 1940 to construct a prisoner of war camp at Victoria.

Two hundred thousand dollars were to be spent on the construction of the prison camp and when finished it would provide work for a staff of 177 people. Government officials were elated over the proposal because the project would pump money into a depressed economy where unemployment was high.

The site chosen was ideal for security: it was not visible from the sea and could only be reached by a narrow road from Carbonear.

Construction workers were hired and began their work. Government went on a spending spree purchasing dishes, stoves, bedding, cutlery, and tents for the prison camp. When finished, it was planned to move one thousand Germans into it. As work progressed, additional meetings were held between Newfoundland and British officials and a decision was made to send captured German Air Force prisoners instead of German civilians.

When the Americans learned of this plan, they were extremely concerned. The 'Yanks' felt that the presence of one thousand trained airmen (Germans) in Newfoundland would cause the Germans to take great risks to rescue them. If during such an effort,

Newfoundland were to be captured by the enemy, the security of the whole of North America would be threatened. Pressure from the American government caused the Newfoundland government to order a halt to the project, and the building was demolished.

The markings for the camp are still visible near the area when the Victoria Lions Club hold their annual demolition derby.

Penni Clarke is to be congratulated for a very fine effort. She has added a great story to the many colourful tales from Newfoundland's past.

This photo taken at Victoria shows the site on which construction had started to build a prison camp to house Nazi war prisoners.

Photo — Jack Fitzgerald

Beaumont Hamel

The Royal Newfoundland Regiment was part of the British 29th Division during the Battle of Beaumont Hamel in World War I. On July 1, 1916 the combined British and French forces launched a major offensive against the Germans, covering a 60 mile front near the river Somme. When the assault ended and the smoke settled, the allies had suffered 19,240 casualties with an additional 38,230 men being wounded.

The offensive started at 8:45 a.m. on July 1, when the Royal Newfoundland Regiment received the order to advance. The 800 Newfoundlanders were required to cross 250 yards, under heavy fire, before even reaching their own front line. At 9:15 a.m. the troops were on the front line and were moving to cross the first of four barbed-wire barricades. They advanced through heavy gunfire past their first obstacle. Casualties were not high at this stage, but as they struggled to the second and then the third obstacle, the casualties increased. The A and B Companies of the Newfoundland Regiment moved steadily ahead followed by C and D company, at intervals of 100 yards.

The first 500 went overseas on the Florizel. This photo shows the Florizel at anchor in St. John's.

Courtesy — Provincial Archives, Nfld.

151

The German guns were bombarding the area over which the Newfoundlanders were advancing and the Newfoundlanders were alone in receiving the full brunt of the enemy fire. It seemed impossible for anyone to survive the terrible inferno sweeping over no-man's-land. Yet the defiant troops from Newfoundland continued down the slopes towards the German guns. By now, casualties were at their highest, and very few managed to reach the German barbed-wire defenses. Most of those at the barbed-wire were shot as they tried to cut through a passage. From start to finish the advance lasted only thirty minutes. On July 2, at roll call only 68 Newfoundlanders responded. Their battalion was virtually annihilated.

In honour of the memory of those gallant men who paid the supreme sacrifice for their country, the Parliament of Newfoundland decreed that the Sunday closest to July 1 be observed as Remembrance Day. The first such Remembrance Day was observed on Sunday, July 1, 1917.

Gas-Mask Inventor

On April 22, 1915 the Germans unleashed great clouds of lethal chlorine gas which quickly spread over French soldiers at the Ypres battlefield. Before the cloud lifted, 5,000 soldiers had died and 10,000 others were left too sick to fight.

This was followed by a similar attack two days later on Canadian troops. The Allies were concerned over this new method of warfare and felt they had to find a defense against it as quickly as possible.

A young Newfoundlander with the Royal Newfoundland Regiment so impressed authorities with his ideas on a new gas mask that the British had him sent to London to work on the anti-gas project. When the mask was ready he allowed himself to be gassed in order to test its effectiveness. The result was the world-famous MacPherson gas-mask which is credited with saving tens of thousands of lives. MacPherson became a legend in his own time.

MacPherson was the son of Campbell MacPherson, founder of the Royal Stores in St. John's. He was born at St. John's, during

March 1879, and was among the first volunteers for the Royal Newfoundland Regiment in 1914. MacPherson saw military action at France, Belgium, Gallipoli, and Egypt. By the time he returned to Newfoundland he was a Lieutenant Colonel.

The British Government sent a special dispatch to the Government of Newfoundland to express its gratitude for his contribution in saving so many lives through his gas-mask invention.

In 1918, King George V made him a Companion of the Order of St. Michael's and St. George. For his work with the St. John Ambulance, he was made a Knight of Grace of the venerable Order of St. John of Jerusalem.

MacPherson's invention brought honour to his native Newfoundland. The world-famous Doctor passed away at St. John's during November 1966 and was laid to rest at the General Protestant Cemetery on Waterford Bridge Road.

Chapter XI
PIRATES

In my book, *Jack Fitzgerald's Notebook* I related many tales of pirates and treasures throughout Newfoundland. These stories included: Peter Eason, Captain Henry Mannering, Eric and Maria Cobham, and Captain John Mason.

This chapter deals with two little known but fascinating pirates: Captain John Philips and Captain Jacob Everson; a pirate kidnapping at Hawe's Point; and a mysterious treasure ship near Baccalieu.

John Philips
The Most Important Pirate
Kidnapped by Pirates
Mystery Ship

John Philips

John Philips set out from England in the 18th century, for Placentia, to seek work as a shipbuilder. Two years later he was the terror of the Atlantic, and a very wealthy man. His decline came even more rapidly than his success. While enroute to Newfoundland, the ship on which he travelled was captured by pirates and Philips was impressed into their crew.

The pirate captain was a blood thirsty villain named Ansis. He tortured prisoners before tossing them to the sharks. Any women taken prisoner were raped and then murdered. Less than a year after being impressed into piracy, Philips was released when Ansis and his followers petitioned for, and were granted, a pardon.

Philips went to Newfoundland but, unable to find work, went on to St. Pierre. He managed to get a job on a fishing boat, but the fishermen in the 18th century were indentured servants, with status little better than that of slaves.

Having seen how easily pirates accumulated wealth, Philips recruited his fellow-workers and captured a ship at St. Pierre, which they called the *Revenge*. In just eight months, Captain Philips was a wealthy pirate captain, having captured thirty-three ships; several of them armed and fitted for war with guns. Five of the captured vessels were turned into pirate ships under Philips' command.

Among the new pirates serving under Philips, were John Rose Archer, a former associate of the notorious Blackbeard (who had been killed on board a British man-o-war five years earlier), and John Fillmore, who had been tried for piracy in Boston, but escaped the gallows. Fillmore was the great-grandfather of the thirteenth president of the United States, Millard Fillmore.

Philips' decline began when he captured a New England ship commanded by Andrew Haradin and impressed Haradin into his crew. Within three days, Haradin plotted a mutiny. He arranged for all the carpenter's tools to be moved on deck where repairs were being made, and upon being given a signal by Haradin, the mutineers grabbed hammers, mallets, and axes, and attacked their pirate captors.

Several pirates were tossed into the sea and their screams awoke Philips, who rushed to the deck only to be axed to death by Haradin. John Rose Archer was also beaten to death. Haradin cut off Captain Philips' head and put it on the yardarm. When he arrived in Boston, the head was soaked in pickle and put on public display. The other pirates were tried and hanged. William Taylor, an Englishman, who had been on his way to Virginia to be sold into slavery to settle a debt in England when he was impressed by Philips, was set free. He returned to Newfoundland where he settled and raised a family.

The Most Important Pirate

One of the most important, but least-known pirates in Newfoundland history was Captain Jacob Everson. Everson had a real effect on Newfoundland history because it was his threat to attack and plunder the city of St. John's that resulted in the first defense organization being set up to protect the harbour and the city.

It was during 1673 that Everson, a Dutch privateer with four armed ships under his command, appeared at the entrance to St. John's Harbour. At the time, Captain Chris Martin, a Devonshire fisherman who was the fishing admiral in the port, proved to be a tough opponent for the pirates.

Captain Martin took guns from the ships in port and placed them at the Narrows. While most historical references to Martin's gallant defense of St. John's claim he had fought off the Dutch with only 23 men, it is more likely that he had a much larger group of fighters with him.

In early accounts of that period, fishing masters only were mentioned in records, with no mention of the servants. With 23 masters under him, Martin likely had a few hundred fighters behind him.

At any rate, Martin succeeded in fighting off Everson's attack and the small pirate fleet left Newfoundland. Eight years later, the pirate captain again met his match, in the person of Captain Henry Morgan, one-time buccaneer, who by that time had become Governor of Jamaica. When Captain Morgan learned that Captain

Everson and a crew of English and Newfoundland pirates were off the Jamaican coast, Morgan recruited a group of fifty men, and, under the cover of darkness, took the pirates by surprise. Most of the crew were captured, tried, and hanged. Everson, and a few others, managed to swim to shore and were never heard from again.

Kidnapped by Pirates

During the 18th century, Newfoundland was a real frontierland. Along with the harsh climate, Indians and many French invasions, the local settlers were in constant danger from pirate attacks. Hawe's Point at Brigus was one place where pirates left their mark. It was a fine summer's day in the early 1700s when a large sailing ship sailed into Hawe's Point and anchored a few hundred feet offshore.

John Hawe was chopping wood outside his home; his wife was inside preparing dinner; and his three children were outside playing. When Hawe viewed the ship, he thought it might be in trouble, so he got in his rowboat and went out to offer help. His wife and three children watched from shore as he climbed aboard the vessel and was being welcomed aboard.

Hawe's family then went on with their activities, expecting his return at any time. Three hours later, they watched as the vessel picked up anchor and sailed out to sea. There was no sign of either John or his little boat.

The vessel was a pirate ship and John, like many other Newfoundlanders in isolated communities had been kidnapped and forced into piracy.

John was heartbroken at the separation from his family and vowed to return to them. He made several attempts to escape, but was recaptured and punished each time. It was twenty years before John Hawe managed to get out of the life of piracy. The pirate captain had abandoned his crew in South America, and John took the opportunity to head back to Newfoundland.

This was difficult, because he had no proper discharge papers. Had he been captured he could have been tried and executed for piracy. It took Hawe two years to work his way to New York, which was still a British port. From there, he got a ship to St.

John's and then another to Brigus.

As John approached the front door of the house he had left twenty years before, he had no idea what to expect. Had his family moved? Had any or all of them died? Hawe was elated when his wife answered the door. It did not take long to convince her who he was, and there was a joyous reunion celebration at Hawe's Point that night.

Mystery Ship

Baccalieu Island has been the site of several discoveries of gold treasure. This story deals with the mysterious circumstances that put a fortune in the hands of a few local fishermen.

During the early 19th century, people living on the north side of Conception Bay were puzzled by the presence of a large brig circling near Baccalieu Island. The curiosity arose because the brig had a suspicious appearance. It was well-armed, had painted ports, and was flying a flag that was completely unknown to the residents in the area.

At night a sudden storm struck from the east north east and gradually increased into a full-blown hurricane. People on shore knew the mystery ship was in trouble after hearing guns being fired and seeing lighted signals of distress, but those on shore were helpless and had to wait for the storm to subside the following morning. A search of the area turned up no trace of the vessel. The incident was a nine-day wonder and was then forgotten. Some time later, a party of hunters sailed to Baccalieu Island to shoot some seabirds. Pulling into Brewster Cove, they discovered several iron kegs lying in the water. When they got the kegs back to their community and opened them, they were found to be filled with sawdust. One of the men, angry over the hard work he had put into getting the kegs from the water, tipped one over deliberately.

To the amazement of all present, several bags emerged from the sawdust. Each keg produced the same, and each bag was tied with a different coloured ribbon and contained paper money.

When government authorities in St. John's learned of the discovery, they sent out several officials. The officials claimed the money for the government and returned a fairly large portion to the finders. One of the men purchased a square-rigged sealing vessel.

People still believe that there is much more treasure lying in the waters around Baccalieu.

Chapter XII
MISCELLANEOUS

The Doyle Bulletin

It is hard to imagine today how a simple nightly radio bulletin could have become a Newfoundland institution for more than thirty years and important enough to be seriously discussed when the terms of Newfoundland's union with Canada were being decided, — but that is exactly what happened with the famous radio show known as the *Doyle Bulletin*.

The *Doyle Bulletin* was initiated in 1922 by businessman Gerald S. Doyle, who saw the need for something to draw the 1200 communities throughout Newfoundland and Labrador closer together. At the time, Doyle was only 27 years old and had the agency for Dr. Chase's patent medicines. He travelled all over Newfoundland, building up his business, an experience that instilled in him the desire to do something for the people he served.

The *Doyle Bulletin* first went on the air November 18, 1922, with William Galgay as the host announcer. At the time of Confederation, the *Doyle Bulletin* was the longest continuously running radio program in all Canada.

To get the show off the ground, Doyle posted notices in telegraph offices throughout Newfoundland and Labrador, inviting people to send their messages and announcements collect to him in St. John's. In no time, the *Doyle Bulletin* was receiving up to 120 messages per day. The program became so popular that it went from a single edition show to two shows per day.

When Joey Smallwood was negotiating terms of union with Canada, one of the items discussed was the continuation of the *Doyle Bulletin* by the CBC, which did not carry commercially sponsored newscasts. An agreement was reached and the show continued.

Gerald S. Doyle passed away on July 12, 1956. Galgay described him as "a most unusual man and a staunch booster of Newfoundland as well as being without peer in his particular brand of advertising." Doyle loved Newfoundland and had on display in his office a glass case containing a reproduction of a scene at the ice. On the walls he displayed many models of Newfoundland steamers and vessels.

Doyle also travelled all over Newfoundland to collect and preserve some of our most popular songs and ballads. During the early years of the *Bulletin*, most Newfoundlanders had battery operated radios. Many of these would be turned on only to hear the *Doyle Bulletin*, then turned off to preserve the batteries.

The last edition of the *Doyle Bulletin* was gathered and written by Gerald S. Doyle's youngest son Patrick, who is now a journalist with the *Evening Telegram*.

Fore and Aft Hats

For a few years during the early part of this century, it was not unusual to see fishermen from the Southern Shore at the squid jigging ground wearing tall Irish-style silk hats. As a matter of fact, it was from these silk hats that the fore and aft hat developed.

The tradition actually started when Richard Sullivan of Ferryland inherited the estate of his Irish father, a Dublin milliner. Included in the estate was a large crate which was too big to move from the wharf at Ferryland. So Sullivan, with the help of fishermen tore open the crate on the dock. There were all sorts of drapes and material and a large supply of tall silk hats. Sullivan gave the hats to the fishermen and they wore them during work, even while jigging squid.

Some cut the hats down four inches and resewed the tops. Others cut the brims off and wore only the high crowns. Yet others cut the sides off, leaving only the front and back parts on; these became known as 'fore and afts'.

Richard's son Jim went on to become a member of the North West Mounted Police and later fought in the Spanish American war.

The Nancys

Newfoundland has played a major role in the history of world aviation. While the famous flight of Alcock and Browne has been immortalized in history, not so well known is the great effort of the U.S. Navy involving a fleet of four planes called the *Nancy 1*, *Nancy 2*, *Nancy 3* and *Nancy 4*.

In 1913, the challenge to hopeful aviators was thrown out by the *London Daily Mail*, which offered 10,000 pounds to the crew of the first plane to make the flight in either direction between the North American continent and any point in Great Britain, or Ireland. Plans by the British, American, French, and Italian aviators to try crossing were interrupted by the First World War. Towards the end of the war, the U.S. Navy was experimenting with long-range flying boats to engage in anti-submarine warfare. The Navy commissioned the world-famous aviation expert Glen Curtis to design the planes.

With the war over, the flyers and designers of the seaplanes began to look seriously at the *Daily Mail* prize. However, the contest rules had changed, and it was now to be a non-stop ocean flight. This ruled out the American effort. The Americans went ahead with their plans to cross the Atlantic purely as a prestige effort.

The *Nancy 2* crashed, and its parts were used for the *Nancy 1*. During May 1919, U.S. man-o-wars and supply vessels were stationed every fifty miles along the course of the planned flight. They even arranged for the destroyers to pour oil on the water to keep down the waves in the event the planes crashed into the sea.

The C-5, a U.S. Navy blimp, was flown to St. John's by Admiral Byrd, who was to fly it across the Atlantic with the seaplanes; but the C-5 broke from its moorings and blew out to sea and was never seen again. Byrd returned to the U.S.

The three *Nancy*s left Long Island on May 10, 1919. The *Nancy 4* was forced down off Boston and had to return to land. The others reached Trepassey on May 14 and were later joined by the *Nancy 4*. On May 16, they set out in their historic trip from Trepassey.

167

The *Nancy 1* crashed and sank west of the Azores. The crew was rescued.

The *Nancy 3* made it to Ponta Delgada after being forced down because of engine trouble.

The *Nancy 4* became the first aircraft to successfully cross the Atlantic, landing in Horta in the Azores.

The *Nancy 4* was nearly shot down accidentally by American guns which were firing into the air as a guide to the location of the landing-site.

The success of the *Nancy 4*, commanded by Albert Read, was later overshadowed by the non-stop crossing of Alcock and Browne.

Sir Robert Bond

Sir Robert Bond, who became prime minister of Newfoundland in 1900 is not only regarded as Newfoundland's greatest statesman, but is perhaps the most unselfish and patriotic man ever to enter public life in this country.

In 1895, Newfoundland was on the brink of financial disaster. Due to economic conditions, Newfoundland was forced to seriously consider confederation with Canada. Negotiations took place, but the Newfoundland delegation felt that Canada's only intention was to exploit this country. Bond, who was then Colonial Secretary, pledged his own personal fortune to guarantee a large loan that saved the country from economic collapse. Bond obviously loved and had great faith in Newfoundland.

As a politician, he was an outstanding figure. In 1890 he succeeded in doing something the Canadian government had been trying for years without success. He successfully negotiated with the United States the famous Bond-Blaine Treaty. The treaty covered a mutual trade agreement between Newfoundland and the United States and provided the U.S. with fishing rights in Newfoundland.

When Ottawa learned of Bond's success, they feared the agreement would make Newfoundland's economy successful and kill all chances of her becoming a Canadian province. The government therefore set out to destroy the Bond-Blaine agreement. The agreement had to be ratified by the British House of Commons, so the Canadians bombarded London with protests.

They presented the deal as an attack on Canadian independence and argued that the treaty would cause great unrest in the Maritime provinces. Bond argued that the Canadian government was interfering in Newfoundland's affairs. the British, however, sided with the Canadian government, and the treaty was not ratified.

It was Bond who settled the French Shore question by having the French fishing rights in Newfoundland nullified. Following that success, he won 32 of 36 seats in a general election. In 1909, Bond was defeated by Sir Edward Morris, leader of the People's Party. The Bank of Montreal, Canadian Iron Ore Company, and the Reids favoured confederation and sided with Morris. After his electoral defeat, he retired from politics. He settled on his estate, the Grange, at Whitbourne, and refused all further attempts to get him back into politics.

Who Owns Labrador?

Who really owns Labrador? Newfoundland? Quebec? Or the descendants of Joseph de la Penha? And who was Joseph de la Penha?

Joseph de la Penha was a wealthy merchant of Holland. He was actually a Spaniard, but fled his country to avoid the Inquisition. When William, Prince of Orange, was formulating plans to raise an army and depose King James II, de la Penha made a handsome contribution to the effort. The money enabled William to capture the English throne and he became indebted to Joseph de la Penha.

To show his gratitude, King William gave title of Labrador to Joseph. The grant, signed in 1697 at the Palace of the Prince of Orange gave de la Penha all the lands, woods, forests, rivers, fruits, and fisheries of Labrador in perpetual or immortal tenure. The grant was renewed several times by the British but de la Penha and his descendants made absolutely no effort to develop their possession.

Not until 1920 was any real interest shown in the grant. In

that year, Isaac de la Penha, a native of Holland, and a Rabbi in Montreal revived the issue. Through his efforts, family members confirmed the grant by King William to the family. A search of the archives of the Netherlands Treasury turned up the copy of the famous grant. The de la Penhas lost their estate and wealth when the Nazi armies invaded Holland.

Again the issue disappeared, only to resurface in 1950, when a group formed the *Association of Labrador*, which attempted to claim Labrador for the de la Penhas. The group set up its headquarters in Amsterdam, Holland, but this too disappeared in time.

The most recent attempt was made in the late 1970s, but that failed also, and Labrador remains part of the Province of Newfoundland and Labrador.

The Petipas Despot

S. J. Benjamin, a writer for an American national magazine called the *Century*, spent his 1883 vacation travelling along the Newfoundland coast on a schooner, the *Alice May* . He was so fascinated by the little community known as Petipas at Little Bay Islands, and the man who ruled the hamlet like a tyrant, that he wrote a series of feature articles which appeared in Newfoundland papers as well as his own magazine.

Benjamin wrote: 'A small place like Petipas always has its leading citizen who acts the part of uncrowned chief. In this case it is Mr. Carter. His will is the law.' Benjamin's article sheds some light on what life in rural Newfoundland communities was like during the 19th century.

When Benjamin visited Carter's General Store, Carter asked, "Have you seen our police force. Well here it is!" and suiting the action to the word, he drew out a massive piece of rope, tarred and four feet in length, which he brought down across the counter with a resounding blow.

"Manys the time I had to use that, when the store's been full of fishermen, sailors, half-breeds, and Indians; all drunk and full of devilry. There was no authority to call upon to keep the peace, and I had to lay about this bit of rope to clear the room by hitting left and right."

Benjamin noted, 'Carter is a typical example of the local despot, exactly fitted to rule among the desperate characters with whom he has to deal. Probably such a ruler is better than none in an isolated place like this.'

Benjamin was also intrigued by the community itself. Unlike the planned and organized streets he was used to, Benjamin wrote, 'Petipas has no streets. It simply consists of an aggregation of houses perched here and there wherever a foothold could be obtained among the rocky ledges which comprise the precipitous hill and which the hamlet has found lodgement.'

The writer concluded that, 'Carter, by force of character, had succeeded in getting the business of the place mostly for his own hands; and the poor who form by far the largest number in such a community, look to him for advances and supplies which result in them being placed shrewdly in his power.'

This system of merchant rule in an outport community which so fascinated the American writer was common throughout Newfoundland at the time.

Cormack

The first white man to walk across Newfoundland was William Epps Cormack, who made the historic trek from Random, Trinity Bay to St. George's Bay during 1822. Cormack was born at St. John's in 1796, the son of a wealthy city merchant. He was educated in Scotland where the famous Scottish mineralogist, Professor Robert Jamieson, inspired him with an enthusiasm for natural history.

At the time Cormack undertook the great challenge, no white man had ever entered the interior from Newfoundland's extreme east coast and emerged on the west coast or vice versa. Cormack had two purposes in mind when he undertook his great adventure. First he wanted to gather detailed information on the minerals and vegetation of the unexplored country; and second, he wanted to make contact with the vanishing Beothuck race.

To prepare for the challenge, the twenty-six-year-old Cormack trained by walking from St. John's to Placentia Bay by way of

Trinity and Conception Bays, a circuit of about 150 miles. Another well-known Newfoundlander, Charles Fox Bennett was scheduled to make the trip with Cormack, but, because he was a magistrate, he could not leave his post. Bennett went on to found the Bennett Brewing Company and to become Prime Minister of Newfoundland.

Cormack actually started at St. John's on August 20, 1822 when he and his Micmac guide, Joseph Sylvester sailed from St. John's for Random Sound, where they planned on starting the long walk. The walk was a difficult ordeal and at one point Cormack had to offer Sylvester a trip to England in order to persuade him from quitting the project. The interior of Newfoundland was rugged. There were many rivers, lakes, hills, and boglands to cross, and the two men often constructed makeshift rafts to cross the water.

When the cold weather set in and snow began falling, the hardships increased. While they failed to meet up with any Beothucks, they did meet and camp with several bands of Micmac Indians. Finally, 59 days after they had started, Cormack and Sylvester walked into St. George's Bay and were welcomed by English and Jersey settlers.

Cormack's activities were not confined to Newfoundland. He played a key role in the settlement of New Glascow; cultivated tobacco in Australia; and was engaged in extensive farming operations in New Zealand. In the British Museum in London there is a treatise by Cormack on scientific skating. He later spent time in California, but spent his last years in British Columbia, where he died in 1868.

The Cross of St. Patrick

The cross of St. Patrick first appeared in Ireland during Cromwell's conquest. Some people will be surprised to learn that there is no tradition in Ireland of a cross of St. Patrick. According to the Irish Heraldic Office in Dublin, St. Patrick was not a martyr, so he is not entitled to a cross as his symbol.

The Irish have never used the cross of St. Patrick as a symbol. Cromwell introduced it in his flag, the Commonwealth Jack, which was made up of the cross of St. George, a gold harp, and the cross of St. Patrick. The cross originated in the arms of the powerful family of the Geraldines, who were representatives in Ireland for King Henry II when he was trying to subjugate the country.

Ireland's traditional emblem was either the shamrock or the harp. It was Cromwell's intention to break with Irish traditions. To do this he took the cross from the badge of the Fitzgeralds and proclaimed it the emblem of Ireland. It was a phoney symbol but at the time Cromwell introduced it, the Irish were in no position to protest.

According to the Newfoundland Historic Society, the ancient symbol for Ireland was the harp. Constantine Chlorus pacified Ireland in 301. In testimony to his success, he adopted the harp of the pagan Irish goddess Hibernia as the insignia on his standard. It remained the badge of Ireland until the time of King Henry II in 1172, when three gold crowns set upon a blue ground was adopted as the Irish flag. The three crowns were eventually replaced once more by the ancient harp of Hibernia.

The red saltire cross on a white ground, emblem of the Fitzgeralds, was never recognized by the Irish as a national flag, but was used as the Irish flag at Cromwell's funeral and later found its way into the Union Jack.

The Fitzgeralds, who had always been loyal to England, became dissatisfied with the English and rebellion resulted. Lord Edward Fitzgerald, husband of Pamela Sims of Fogo, was killed in that rebellion. The rising of the United Irishmen was put down and Britain felt it would be safer to unite it with England and Scotland. Claiming the rising had proven that the Irish parliament was incompetent, the British convinced the Anglo-Irish parliament to join in union with Britain. A majority of 21 votes out of 303 members won the day for England, but the bitterness caused by it had not yet been resolved.